I0572622

First Published in the United States of America in 2024 by the Louisville Urban League
1535 W Broadway
Louisville, KY 40203
Phone: (502) 585-4622
www.lul.org

ISBN 978-0-9998831-5-0

Digital edition published in 2024

Cover photo: Daphne Walker

Photography:
Individual Artists

Design:
Daphne Walker: dwalker@lul.org
Mya Davidson: designsxmya.com

Louisville Urban League 2024

STATE OF BLACK LOUISVILLE

TABLE OF

INTRODUCTION 06
LYNDON E. PRYOR

It's Always Halloween — 08
LYNDON PRYOR

JOBS 11

Investment in Black Workers Is Critical to Construction Workforce — 12
MICHAEL GRITTON

A Housing Crisis Masquerading as a Workforce Problem — 14
RA'SHANN MARTIN

The Inclusion of DEI and Supplier Diversity Efforts — 16
TRAVIS FOXX

JUSTICE 19

The More Things Change — 20
DR. ERIC T. FRENCH

The 2024 Legislative Session and the State of Black Louisville — 23
JACKIE MCGRANAHAN

When Injustice Becomes Law, Rebellion Becomes Duty: How Coalition Building is Necessary to Sustain Our Commonwealth — 28
DR. KAILA ADIA STORY

Key Takeaways from The History of Policing in Louisville: A Fact-Finding Report on Institutional Harms — 30
FELICIA JAMISON, PH.D.
SIDDHANT ISSAR, PH.D.
CATHERINE FOSL, PH.D
MYA TODD
ETHAN GORTON
ISABELLA JOHNSON
CHERIE DAWSON-EDWARDS PH.D.

The State of White Allyship in Black Louisville — 34
CHRISTINA SHADLE

The Louisville Metro Police Department Must Do Better for Black People — 36
SHAMEKA PARRISH-WRIGHT

What Happens? — 38
SADIQA N. REYNOLDS, ESQ.

EDUCATION 41

Future Focus of Racial Equity — 42
BJ BUNTON

HBCUs are Imperative to Black Progress; They Need Financial Support from Liberal Allies — 44
DR. KEVIN COSBY

Black Students Can and Will Learn at Grace James and DuBois Academies — 49
DR. LATONYA FRAZIER
DR. MONICA HUNTER

The Necessity of Black Student Activism and Unions in Public Schools — 54
GREG VANN AND
AMAYA WILLIAMS

As It Relates — Black Louisville and Racial Equity: The Less and More of the Racial Equity Policy — 56
JOHN DAVID MARSHALL

CONTENTS

The State of the District 2024 — 58
DR. CORRIE SHULL

Anti-Racist and White: What DEP Offers to Address White Supremacy — 60
RACHEL KLEIN

Dedication to Diane Porter — 64
JOHN DAVID MARSHALL

HEALTH 67

Food Justice And Farming in Louisville — 68
LOUISVILLE URBAN LEAGUE'S TEAM KILIMO

Parenting While Black — 70
DR. ARMON R. PERRY AND DR. CHERI LANGLEY

The State of Environmental Justice — 74
EBONI COCHRAN

HOUSING 77

1954 to 2024: On the 70th Anniversary of the Wade-Braden Case — 78
ANGELA STOREY, PH.D.

Louisville Needs More Housing Diversity — 80
TONY CURTIS AND CASSIA HERRON

Redressing Wealth Disparities Caused by Institutional Racism in Housing — 84
JOHN D. BORDERS, JR.

The Fair Housing Act is Not Working — 87
NATALIE HARRIS

BLACK BUSINESS 89

Accelerators Are Not Enough to Address Black Wealth Disparities — 90
DANA J. JOHNSON

Louisville Must Grow Our Economy Through Education, Emphasizing Business Opportunities and Future Workforce — 92
DELQUAN DORSEY

Investing in the Future of Black Business — 94
CYNTHIA BROWN

The Importance of Economic Power in the Black Community — 96
DAVE W. CHRISTOPHER, SR.

FURTHER REFLECTIONS 99

A Demonstration of Philanthropy and Black Communities as Strategic Partners and Champions for Transformative Change — 100
RAMONA DALLUM

The Conviction to Champion Equity: Philanthropy's Role in Empowering Leaders of Color Metro United Way — 103
ADRIA JOHNSON

INTRODUCTION

LYNDON E. PRYOR
President & CEO, Louisville Urban League

"To be black and conscious in America is to be in a constant state of rage." — James Baldwin

In a time when many would rather ignore the realities of our racialized society, the Louisville Urban League's biennial publication, "State *of Black Louisville*", stands as a beacon of truth and a testament to the resilience of the Black community. This report offers a comprehensive look at the challenges and triumphs faced by Black Louisvillians, providing critical insights and data that are often overlooked or suppressed.

"*State of Black Louisville*" centers Black people, Black stories, and Black data, shedding light on a historically marginalized community's unique experiences and perspectives. The 2024 edition of this essential publication takes on added significance in the wake of the 2024 election, which saw a rise in political rhetoric that sought to divide and ignore the concerns of Black voters.

Now more than ever, it is essential to have a resource that provides accurate and nuanced information about the state of Black Louisville. The Louisville Urban League's commitment to uplifting Black voices and amplifying Black data is eternal, and this publication serves as a vital tool for

policymakers, community leaders, and all who seek to understand the complexities of race and equity in our city.
As you embark on a journey through the profound essays in the pages that follow, you will find a treasure trove of wisdom, knowledge, inspiration, and cautionary tales. However, above all, I fervently hope you find an abundance of courage.

Courage is the catalyst that propels us to challenge the status quo, to question the narratives that have been imposed upon us, and to stand steadfastly for what is right, even when the path ahead seems daunting. The essays within this publication serve as a reminder that the struggle for racial justice remains an ongoing endeavor. The road to achieving true freedom and equality for all is still fraught with obstacles. Still, I firmly believe that by uniting and working in concert, we can forge a better future for ourselves and for generations to come.

I implore you to approach these essays with an open heart and a curious mind. Allow the stories and experiences of the contributors to stir your soul. Let their indomitable courage inspire you to play your part in creating a society where justice and equity prevail for all.

James Baldwin said, "You write in order to change the world, knowing perfectly well that you probably can't, but also knowing that literature is indispensable to the world." The essays of "*State of Black Louisville*" will not alone change the world. Still, they do have the potential to ignite a transformative spark within us, empowering us to embrace our collective responsibility and work tirelessly towards a world where the rights and dignity of all individuals are upheld.
As you delve into these pages, may you find the courage to challenge injustice, amplify marginalized voices, and advocate for a future where equality and compassion flourish, for it is through our unified efforts and unwavering commitment that we will ultimately create a world where every person — regardless of race or circumstance — can live with dignity and boundless possibilities.

IT'S ALWAYS HALLOWEEN

LYNDON E. PRYOR
President & CEO, Louisville Urban League

In John Carpenter's "*Halloween*" (1978), the world is introduced to Michael Myers, a deranged madman who unleashes terror on the small town of Haddonfield, Illinois every October 31. Myers has withstood the unimaginable for 44 years. Through thirteen films, he's continued his reign of death and destruction. He has been jailed, stabbed, shot, burned, blown up, and even decapitated, and despite it all, he just keeps coming. That is the slasher film series's running theme: no matter what, if it's Halloween, Michael Myers is coming.

Those of us who believe in social and economic equity and racial progress in this country, and who seek to preserve the progress that has been made, would do well to learn from the example of Myers' victims. Most of his victims, despite their many experiences to the contrary, insist on believing Michael isn't coming "this" Halloween. And, almost without fail, those who are unprepared perish. Because if it is Halloween, Michael Myers is coming. For those of us who believe in social and economic equity and racial progress, white supremacy, classism, and racialized capitalism are Michael Myers — and it's always Halloween.

After the Civil War, southerners and white supremacists took several steps to reassert their dominance and circumvent the outcomes of the conflict, particularly the abolition of slavery and the rights granted to African Americans during Reconstruction. To do so, they employed some critical actions.

Immediately after the Civil War, many southern states enacted the Black Codes — laws aimed at restricting the freedom of Black people and ensuring their availability as a cheap labor force. These laws severely limited civil rights and curtailed economic opportunity. Through the Compromise of 1877, southern Democrats agreed to support Rutherford B. Hayes as president in exchange for the withdrawal of federal troops from the South, effectively ending Reconstruction. This allowed southern states to implement discriminatory practices without federal intervention.

Michael Myers is always coming.

At that same time and persisting well into the 21st century, groups like the Ku Klux Klan (KKK) and other white supremacist organizations used terror, violence, and intimidation to suppress Black political participation and social movement. This included the use of lynchings, beatings, and threats against those who attempted to exercise their new rights. Jim Crow laws and zoning guidelines like redlining mandated racial segregation and governed social mobility and economic investments across entire regions of both the North and South. These laws reinforced white supremacy and systemically disenfranchised Black communities.

It is always Halloween.

Though they have morphed and grown appendages, the relics of these programs are alive and well today. They are built into a "justice" system that punishes Black and Brown people at rates far disproportionate to their white counterparts for the same offenses. In 2022, Black people were admitted to jails at four times the rate of white people.[1] Black men in the federal system receive sentences that are nearly 20% longer than those of white men convicted of similar crimes.[2] Black defendants are more likely to be offered plea deals that include jail or prison time.[3] Black people receive higher bail than white people for violent crimes, public order crimes, and drug crimes.[4] Black and Brown juveniles are significantly more likely to come into contact with the justice system than white, non-Hispanic juveniles.[5]

Discrimination is baked into every facet of our economy. According to the Economic Policy Institute, "One of the most durable and defining features of the U.S. labor market is the 2-to-1 disparity in unemployment that exists between Black and white workers… In 2019, the typical (median) black worker earned 24.4% less per hour than the typical white worker. This is an even larger wage gap than in 1979, when it was 16.4%.[6]" Black applicants are 1.8–2.5 times more likely to be denied a mortgage than white applicants with similar characteristics. In 2018–2019, lenders denied 17% of Black applicants, compared to 8% of white applicants.[7] The impact of redlining is still felt throughout the country. Politics and education are not exempt. Voting rights are under attack, with polling locations being closed and voter rolls being purged nationwide. Project 2025 is a detailed plan to diminish voting access for millions[8] and completely eliminate the Department of Education.[9] We see this today in Kentucky as the state Assembly has taken active steps over the last several years to weaken public education, roll back diversity and equity efforts, and disenfranchise Black and poor students. The banning of books and the restrictions on curriculum are only the most recent signs of the wave of anti-intellectualism sweeping across the country, seeking to dumb down society. While we were celebrating the Voting Rights Act of 1965, Brown, and advances in equity, the opposition was plotting and moving to undo it all.

It is always Halloween. Michael Myers is coming.

Before it was co-opted, misused, worn out, and summarily neutered by the masses, "woke" or "stay woke" was simply Black people's way of reminding one another that we cannot stop the fight for progress because those seeking to re-establish white dominance in the social, political, and economic spheres will not stop coming. That does not mean that we cannot or should not rest. Rest is vital to our individual and communal health and well-being. But, there is a difference between rest and retirement. We cannot afford to believe that when we win ground in the fight for freedom and civil liberties, the fight is finished and we can retreat from the battlefield. The assaults on the Voting Rights Act and Roe v. Wade are examples of how the proponents of oppression are always on the offensive. They are Michael Myers and, for them, it's always Halloween.

Our charge is to be vigilant, ever ready, and never forget. Equity is not a destination and something to be achieved. It is an action or a process that we must continually work to perfect and implement. It is a laborious and challenging endeavor, and the opposition is relentless, but we must be creative and intentional. We must collaborate and coordinate among individuals, organizations, and communities to build systems that work for everyone. We have to prepare and invest in the leaders of today and tomorrow so that we can build on our progress and not fight the same battles for generations later. This is not about fear but, rather, the pursuit of freedom and implementing strategic actions. We have an opportunity to build the community and country we deserve — one that embraces justice, equality, and opportunity for all. We can achieve and maintain it if we are unwavering in our collective commitment to do so.

It is always Halloween, and Michael Myers is coming. But we will be prepared.

IN 2022, BLACK PEOPLE WERE ADMITTED TO JAILS AT FOUR TIMES THE RATE OF WHITE PEOPLE.

BLACK MEN IN THE FEDERAL SYSTEM RECEIVE SENTENCES THAT ARE NEARLY 20% LONGER THAN THOSE OF WHITE MEN CONVICTED OF SIMILAR CRIMES.

BLACK DEFENDANTS ARE MORE LIKELY TO BE OFFERED PLEA DEALS THAT INCLUDE JAIL OR PRISON TIME.

BLACK PEOPLE RECEIVE HIGHER BAIL THAN WHITE PEOPLE FOR VIOLENT CRIMES, PUBLIC ORDER CRIMES, AND DRUG CRIMES.

BLACK AND BROWN JUVENILES ARE SIGNIFICANTLY MORE LIKELY TO COME INTO CONTACT WITH THE JUSTICE SYSTEM THAN WHITE, NON-HISPANIC JUVENILES.

JOBS

"DESPITE MAKING UP 13% OF THE REGION'S WORKFORCE, BLACK WORKERS ACCOUNT FOR ONLY 4% OF LOCAL JOBS IN THE CONSTRUCTION INDUSTRY."

MICHAEL GRITTON

INVESTMENT IN BLACK WORKERS IS CRITICAL TO CONSTRUCTION WORKFORCE

MICHAEL GRITTON
Executive Director, KentuckianaWorks

For hundreds of years, white people wrote and enforced laws that made it difficult or impossible for Black people to succeed economically. The legacy of that history can still be seen today in the pervasive systemic inequity that exists in the labor market.

Black workers have higher unemployment rates, lower median earnings, and are more likely to be among the working poor than white workers. Research from the Urban Institute (Biu et al., 2023) shows in detail how workers of color are underrepresented in high-quality jobs, and crowded into low-quality, often low-wage occupations.[1] Ultimately, the researchers found getting a good job depends more on race and gender than education, because regardless of educational attainment, persistent inequities remain in access to quality jobs.

One example of these patterns of occupational segregation can be seen in how Black men and women are crowded out of high-quality jobs in construction, a trend that holds both nationally and locally. Despite making up 13% of the region's workforce, Black workers account for only 4% of local jobs in the construction industry. So, out of the more than 30,000 workers employed in the local construction sector, only 1,200 are Black or African American.

Jobs in the construction trades are attractive positions. They generally do not require a college degree, provide a living wage, and score well on other indicators of job quality including scheduling, benefits, on-the-job training, and union coverage.[2] Average wages for local construction jobs are $26 per hour, north of $54,000 per year.

The region's Workforce Board — called KentuckianaWorks — and the Administration of Governor Andy Beshear have taken action to address this inequity, providing multiple years of funding to the Louisville Urban League to run Kentuckiana Builds, a free training program available to those interested in entering the construction sector. The six-week program lays the foundation for a position as an entry-level construction worker. While open to all applicants, Kentuckiana Builds focuses on recruiting women and Black candidates into the training program, seeking to address the industry's relative lack of diversity.

Graduates of Kentuckiana Builds earn three nationally recognized industry credentials and can access up to 12 hours of dual credit at Jefferson Community and Technical College. The program also awards incentives to students that adhere to employer hiring values including continuous learning, honesty, punctuality, customer service, and quality.

Since its inception in 2016, more than 600 people have completed the Kentuckiana Builds program, with 90% of graduates being people of color and 25% women. The program has placed more than 440 people into employment at an average wage of more than $16 per hour. Many of those graduates have gone on to build successful careers in the construction industry. Some have gone on to work on development sites that will have a long-lasting impact on the fabric of west Louisville, including the Norton Healthcare Sports & Learning Center, Goodwill's West Louisville Opportunity Center, and the forthcoming Norton West Louisville Hospital.

Markitta Ford is one of those 400+ graduates now working in construction. She was raised in the Shawnee neighborhood of west Louisville, where she continues to live today. She graduated from Kentuckiana Builds earlier this year and is now working for HMC at the new Norton West Louisville Hospital site. Markitta said this about her experience:

"As a three-time convicted felon, I never thought in a million years I'd be standing right here... It's a dream come true to me... just having my feet planted in gravel, to be a part of changing the landscape of the city I was born and raised in... I'm building history... This is something we haven't seen in the West End of Louisville in forever, at least not since I was born, and I'm thirty-five."

The Commonwealth has secured a number of infrastructure awards from recent federal funding, some of which can be spent on workforce development. This is a real opportunity to address systems of occupational segregation and , an aging workforce, and produce more prepared candidates for those available jobs in the growing construction sector.

Programs like Kentuckiana Builds have traditionally been funded by the federal government, but Congress' investments in workforce development have been shrinking for many years now. Organizations like KentuckianaWorks and the Louisville Urban League know how to design and run workforce programs that help more disadvantaged workers find quality employment — , but we need additional public investments to do so.

A HOUSING CRISIS MASQUERADING AS A WORKFORCE PROBLEM

RA'SHANN MARTIN
Executive Director, St. John Center

Ah, Louisville.

We affectionately call ourselves a "Compassionate City," but are more widely known as the city of bourbon, horse racing, and now... a severe lack of affordable housing? It's 2024, and here we are still grappling with a crisis that's been brewing longer than a barrel of Pappy Van Winkle. This isn't just about roofs over heads. It's about the very foundation of our community, our economy, and, dare I say, our humanity.

Picture this: 36,000 units. That's not the number of mint juleps served at Derby; it's our affordable housing deficit for low-income renters. Black residents are bearing the brunt of this shortage. Black residents and families are more likely to be "cost-burdened," a polite term for "choosing between rent and dinner." This issue is not unique to Louisville, but reflects a broader national trend where housing affordability and access are increasingly recognized as critical factors in workforce success and economic development.

Our affordable housing crisis directly impacts our workforce problem. When families are forking over more than 30% of their income just to keep a roof over their heads, there's precious little left for those "luxuries" like education, skills training, or – heaven forbid – career advancement.

Not only are we short on affordable housing, but the housing we do have is often very far from where the jobs are. It's like we've created an urban version of "The Amazing Race," where workers have to navigate a labyrinth of long commutes and high transportation costs just to clock in. And let me tell you, 58% of companies report workers citing commute times as a reason for leaving. I mean, who wouldn't want to spend half their waking hours in traffic?

Now, let's talk about the elephant in the room or, rather, the AI in the office. While we're wringing our hands over housing, the corporate world is busy figuring out how to replace humans with algorithms. This trend should be specifically concerning for Black Louisville, as we disproportionately continue to suffer from a digital divide. Efficiency, they call it. I call it a divestment in humanity. But hey, who needs a living wage when you can have a chatbot, right?

At St. John Center, we're on the front lines of this crisis. In fiscal year 2024, we served 3,078 people in our Day Shelter and Social Service Center. Forty-six percent were African American, and 50% of all clients self-reported dealing with mental health issues. If we assume 60% of these individuals are workforce-eligible, we're looking at a minimum of 500-600 Black Louisvillans trying to work but struggling because they don't have a stable place to call home. We know these numbers are modest and only a segment of a much bigger picture.

Home. It's where workers go to sleep at night. It's where they wake up and prepare to be their most productive, highest-functioning selves. But in Louisville, for too many, home is a luxury they can't afford. And let me tell you, a community saturated with fear — fear of homelessness, fear of the unhoused, fear for humanity itself — is not a productive one.

So how does a city solve a housing crisis masquerading as a workforce problem? We need a multi-faceted approach that includes zoning reforms, incentives for developers, and investments in public transportation. Ultimately, Employer Assisted Housing (EAH) programs are the solutions that address both the housing crisis and the workforce problem. While not notably implemented in Louisville, these employer-led initiatives can take various forms, including direct financial assistance for housing, partnerships with nonprofit organizations, on-site housing development, and advocacy for housing-friendly policies. Some companies offer down payment assistance or low-interest loans, while others collaborate with nonprofits to manage housing programs. Large employers in Louisville could contribute significantly to solving both housing and workforce challenges.[1]

As the Executive Director of St. John Center, a homeless service agency working to be a bigger part of the solution, my colleagues and I watch this crisis unfold day after day, year after year. We call on community leaders to invest in affordable housing projects, combat NIMBYism ("Not In My BackYard"), support organizations like St. John Center, advocate for policy changes, promote workforce development programs, and encourage public-private partnerships.

We need to stop treating housing as a privilege and start recognizing it as both a fundamental right and the answer to our workforce problem. Until we address housing as a fundamental need, all our talk about economic mobility and job opportunities is just that – talk.

As we face this challenge, we're tired but not defeated. Housing isn't just a right — it's a fight. And it's one we can't afford to lose. By working together, we can create a future where everyone has access to safe, affordable housing and the opportunity to thrive, ensuring a stronger workforce and more vibrant communities for all.

So, Louisville, it's time to put our money where our mint juleps are. It's time to invest in our people, our communities, and our shared humanity. Because at the end of the day, a house isn't just a structure; it's the foundation for everything else.

THE INCLUSION OF DEI AND SUPPLIER DIVERSITY EFFORTS

TRAVIS FOXX
Vice President of Business Development, Cornerstone Engineering

In my humble opinion, the state of Black Louisville is a microcosm of the state of our country. While there are entities that align themselves with the righteous cause of Diversity, Equity and Inclusion (DEI), there are others that are indifferent to the plight of those who have been historically marginalized. Even worse, there are several that stand on the opposite side of progress. As we bear witness to local educational institutions and commercial enterprises terminating and rolling back their DEI policies, we know this iniquity is occurring simultaneously throughout the nation.

Those who work to terminate DEI efforts are under a gross misconception that the exclusion of Black and minority people and businesses from the table of opportunity is for the betterment of this city and our country. Entities that have no interest in employing or collaborating with people of color are doing their organizations a disservice by depriving their organizations of access to a talent pool filled with some of the most skilled workers and innovative thinkers the world has ever known.

There is also a gaping disparity between entities that state they have an interest in participation and those that are intentional in their efforts to ensure inclusion. We have questions:

- **Just how inclusive are you if the registration that allows companies to conduct business with your entity creates more barriers than it removes?**
- **How inclusive are you when the documentation you distribute to inform individuals of project details is either vague, incomprehensible, or often overwhelming?**
- **How inclusive are you when the qualifications and requirements mandated to perform as a subcontractor on your corporation's projects are well beyond the prerequisites set forth by local municipalities for small firms to legally perform their core competencies?**
- **How inclusive are you when the flyers have gone out, the minority outreaches have been held, there is minimal participation when the project starts, and your report to the owner only states there was a good faith effort put forth to add minority firms as suppliers on the project?**

While these practices may be a bit disheartening, hope lies with those doing the work in the community along with local and federal government. For example, I find hope in the nonprofits and educational institutions that continue to develop programs that ensure scaling of Black firms and the enhancement of skill sets within the Black workforce. I find hope in the local government and utility company personnel who insist upon the creation of initiatives that provide funding for urban development and employment opportunities.

I find hope in federal agencies'inclusion of minimum Minority Business Enterprise (MBE)/ Small Business Enterprise (SBE) participation requirements. Lastly, but most importantly, I find hope in THE PEOPLE. There are Black Louisvillians who won't go quietly into the night and settle for crumbs. Rather, they will demand at city council meetings, community outreaches, and the polling booth that the disparity in opportunity be addressed.

So, when asked my opinion on the state of Black Louisville, my answer is this: Black Louisville is resilient and never wavering. I say to Black-owned firms: Never stop pushing the needle. Let your performance, not just your certification, make it impossible to ignore you. I would say to Black workers: Show up and show out each day, strive to be the best, and never stop improving upon your skill set. I say to commercial enterprises: Step up and ensure more than a **good faith effort** is being made to secure inclusion on your projects. I say to our champions like the Louisville Urban League: Never stop fighting for our community. WE ARE WORTH IT.

I implore each one of these entities in our community to continue lifting each other up through advocacy and patronage.

When you cross paths, by all means, share that salutatory head nod and keep it moving because there is work yet to be done!

> "JUST LIKE MY MAMA, AUNT'S AND UNCLES HAVE SAID, 'MANY BLACK PEOPLE FEEL ALL THEY HAVE TO DO IS **STAY BLACK** AND **DIE.**'"

SHAMEKA PARRISH-WRIGHT

THE MORE THINGS CHANGE

ERIC T. FRENCH
Sr. Pastor, Antioch Baptist Church

In 1849, French writer Jean-Baptiste Alphonse Karr wrote "plus ca change, plus c'est la meme chose," which means "the more things change, the more they stay the same." Those words still ring true 175 years later. Many thought our country had truly changed with the election of the first African American U.S. President in 2008. Some thought America had finally begun to escape the grasp of its long history of slavery and segregation. Unfortunately, little did we realize that a moment that brought such hope to millions would also be the spark that ignited a resurgence of white supremacy and Christian nationalism. The result of this resurgence was the election of a U.S. President in 2016 who continues to fan the flames of division and hatred for his own economic and political benefit. Now, there is a well-organized movement by his delusional disciples and enemies of justice to work through state legislatures across this country to reverse the social and political advancements of the last 60 years. The movement's ultimate goal is to stop any effort to create a more equitable and just society, and return the nation to the separate and unequal despair of the 1950s.

The 2024 Kentucky Legislative Session is a primary example of this unrelenting attack on democracy, truth, common sense, and justice. Some of the bills passed during this session stand in stark contrast to the principles proclaimed in the preamble to our state constitution: We, the people of the Commonwealth of Kentucky, grateful to Almighty God for the civil, political and religious liberties we enjoy, and invoking the continuance of these blessings, do ordain and establish this Constitution."[1] These bills do not demonstrate gratitude to God, but instead an open contempt for God's love, grace, and mercy. True gratitude towards God would be expressed by ensuring that every Kentuckian has the opportunity to experience the blessing of affordable housing, quality education, quality healthcare, a livable wage, and to live without fear of being harmed because of their race, sexuality, or socioeconomic status. Instead, with a 3.4 billion dollar rainy day surplus at its disposal, the Kentucky legislature used its time in Frankfort to pass bills that would lead to a separate and unequal commonwealth.

A quick review of the most egregious of these bills reveals the utter contempt that some in the Legislature have for God and people. For example, House Bill 5 criminalizes homelessness, House Bill 6 removes funding for the Affordable Housing Trust, and House Bill 18 legalizes housing discrimination by allowing landlords to reject Section 8 housing vouchers. In a time when affordable housing is difficult to find, the legislature should be making it easier to find housing, not harder. Rather than using the surplus to lessen the burden of poverty in Kentucky, the legislature took aim at Diversity/Equity/Inclusion programs (HB9, SB9, SB93), Voting Rights (SB6, SB 80), the environment (HB 136, HB 141), Labor Laws (HB 255, HB 500), the City of Louisville (HB388) and JCPS (Concurrent Resolution 81). These bills will be detrimental to the future of our state and particularly harmful to the health and well-being of the African-American community and the poor once they become law.

It is not surprising that we must once again fight against white supremacy and Christian Nationalism — because they never left. They just regrouped. What has been surprising and disheartening is the slow response of the African American church to these attacks. The African American church has historically been the center of strength and faith in the African American community. It has produced prophetic leaders in the fight for civil rights; provided venue space; hosted meetings; supported and attended rallies and marches; and provided emotional, moral, and spiritual support for its congregations. There have been individual members of the clergy and the African American faith community who have demonstrated undeniable courage in speaking out against the moral insanity that has overtaken the state of Kentucky's legislature in Frankfort. But collectively, the response to the social and economic attacks on the African American community has been disorganized and lethargic at best. There has been no mobilization of clergy across denominations, no organizing of the community at large, no collaboration with the Louisville chapter of the National Association for the Advancement of Colored People (NAACP) or the Louisville Urban League, no mass protests, no fiery testimonies before the house and senate committees, no sit-ins at the state capital, no boycotts of companies, no calls to vote politicians out of office, and no confrontation of closed-mouthed liberal allies. We have outrage, but little action.

Let me be clear: I love and believe in the African American church and the God we serve. Critique is not the same as criticism and condemnation. The faithfulness and vitality of the African American church are essential to the future well-being of the African American community and nation. I still believe in the African American church and the hope it represents for our community and commonwealth. I see its human weakness, but I also see its God-given power and promise. The time has come for the African American church to reclaim its prophetic voice. It must declare with one voice, "Woe to those who make unjust laws, to those who issue oppressive decrees to deprive the poor of their rights and withhold justice from the oppressed of my people, making widows their prey and robbing the fatherless (Isaiah 10:1-2)."[2]

It's time for the African American church to boldly expose Jim and Jane Crow Esquire Inc.'s naked aggression toward people of color and the poor. And as important as prophetic preaching is to identify problems, we also need divinely inspired plans to eradicate the problems we face. We have passion, we have preaching, and we have prayer. Now we need plans to create alliances with other people, groups, and organizations facing the same assault from white supremacy and Christian nationalism. We can no longer afford to remain isolated in our silos, dealing with our own denominational and congregational issues. The time has come to place the concerns of the community — sinners and saints alike — above our own needs and concerns. The time has come for us to set aside our petty differences, theological disagreements, and personal agendas. It is time to begin working together. We shall overcome because it is true that the more things change, the more they stay the same. Thankfully, though, God declared, "I the Lord do not change. So you…are not destroyed (Malachi 3:6).[3]

THE 2024 LEGISLATIVE SESSION AND THE STATE OF BLACK LOUISVILLE

JACKIE MCGRANAHAN
Senior Policy Strategist, American Civil Liberties Union of Kentucky

Being Black in Louisville is still a precarious existence. We are facing all the problems that come with existing as minorities in this country, concentrated in the microcosm that is Louisville. We have fought, and continue to fight, for representation in spaces where policy decisions are made. While it continues to be an uphill battle, we claim space and advocate for Black Kentuckians.

The Kentucky General Assembly is responsible for establishing policies to direct the future of everyone in the state, but their policy decisions are often felt more acutely by Black Kentuckians.

BUDGETING, EDUCATION, AND BLACK LOUISVILLE

The even-numbered years of the General Assembly are dominated by budget conversations, as the Kentucky General Assembly drafts, edits, and passes the state budget. This year, Kentucky is in a surplus, partially due to pandemic-era federal dollars. Pre-pandemic, Kentucky received 27.8% of revenue from the federal government, which increased to 32.2% in 2020.[1] The passage of the American Rescue Act and the Infrastructure Act padded those numbers even further.[2] As a result, the Kentucky government is flush with cash but, the question is, where are we spending it?

Investments in education are key to the health and prosperity of our community. Many economists believe if we can improve education overall, our wages, employment, and quality of life will follow. One integral step toward educational funding for Black Kentuckians was included in this year's House budget — additional funding for Kentucky's oldest historically Black university, Kentucky State University (KSU).

For years, KSU has been inequitably underfunded when compared to other Kentucky universities. Last fall, the federal government sent letters to sixteen southern states regarding funding disparities between historically Black land-grant institutions and white land-grant institutions. Senate President Pro-Tempore David Givens said, "Funding to the university is up 200%; we do remain committed to trying to see this institution thrive."[3] We must hold the legislature to the promise of continuing to fund HBCUs equitably.

In one of the first committee hearings of the interim (the period of time from adjournment of the regular session to the convening of the next session), KSU officials gave legislators a progress update on the $23 million granted the university to offset their budget shortfalls. Kentucky State University has completed 41% of the improvement plan objectives, with the majority of the remaining in progress. A new president has taken office, Koffi C. Akakpo, and the university has the largest general fund in its history. The retention rate for students is up, and on track to be at 75% by the fall.[4]

In K-12 education, school transportation was also fully funded in the House budget, at 80% of the statutorily required amount in 2025, and 100% in 2026. Jefferson County Public Schools (JCPS) faced disastrous transportation issues in 2023, which had an outsized impact on Black Louisvillians. Kentucky's largest and most diverse school district is JCPS, with 37.2% of its student population identifying as Black.

Sadly, but not surprisingly, we have seen a wave of legislation targeting diversity, equity, and inclusion (DE&I) in both K-12 schools and institutes of higher education. Senate Bills 6 and 93 as well as House Bills 9 and 224 targeted DE&I in Kentucky schools. Senate Bill 6 was proposed to restrict DE&I efforts in public postsecondary institutions. It would prohibit universities from requiring students or employees to endorse specific ideologies or political viewpoints, particularly "divisive concepts." It would also limit mandatory DE&I training and the use of state funds for DE&I-related activities. This legislation passed quickly out of the Senate. Once the bill reached the House, House Bill 9 was added to the legislation. House bill 9 focuses on charter schools, proposing the establishment of a funding mechanism. This was not an explicitly anti-DE&I measure; diverting funds to charter schools could undermine public school resources and potentially affect DE&I programs.

Senate bill 93 was a more extreme version of the legislation. This bill targeted K-12 public schools. It intended to ban the expenditure of resources on DE&I programs and political or social activism. It also proposed removing references to trauma-informed approaches from state law, arguing that such language could indirectly support a DE&I agenda. House bill 224 sought to amend existing education statutes, including provisions relating to curriculum content and instruction materials. This bill aimed to ensure that educational content adhered to certain standards, which some interpreted as a move to limit DE&I-related teachings. Legislators attempted to find agreement on the legislation but, ultimately, ran out of time. No version of this harmful legislation passed.

Dismissing inequities or legislating Kentuckians' ability to even discuss our differences does not erase racism or bigotry; it just sends a message to Black, Brown, and LGBTQ Kentuckians that we're moving on and we're going to keep ignoring your concerns.

HEALTHCARE AND THE LEGISLATURE

Healthcare in Kentucky continues to be an issue, especially for Black Kentuckians. Racial disparities are common in many areas of healthcare including diabetes, heart health, and cancer deaths. The disparity between maternal health outcomes for Black and white Kentuckians is stark and can be attributed to several factors, two of which are systemic racism and implicit bias in healthcare.

Racism is part and parcel of being Black in the United States, and it compromises the health of Black families. Black women in Kentucky experience maternal mortality rates approximately twice as high as those of white women. In 2018, the pregnancy-related death rate for Black women was 40.2 per 100,000 live births, compared to 13.1 per 100,000 for white women.[5] The infant mortality rate for Black infants in Kentucky is significantly higher than the infant mortality rate for ANY other racial and ethnic demographic in Kentucky.[6] Physical health risk factors alone cannot account for these disparities.

Addressing maternal health in Kentucky is a complicated endeavor, so the policy initiatives of American Civil Liberties Union of Kentucky (ACLU-KY) are multi-pronged, but focused on four key areas:

1. **Addressing poverty and other socioeconomic factors that contribute to poor maternal health outcomes.**

2. **Pushing policymakers for enhanced maternal health data collection and analysis.**

3. **Investing in community-based solutions, like birthing centers and access to doulas.**

4. **Supporting parents who are incarcerated.**

Legislators acted on promises to address maternal health in the 2024 session. House Bill 10 helps ensure pregnancy is a qualifying event for insurance coverage; set up a hotline to assist healthcare professionals treating new moms who may be suffering from postpartum-related mental illness; and expanded access to HANDS, a publicly administered program that serves new families by increasing access to healthcare, including mental health care. On the final day of session, House Bill 10 was added as an amendment to Senate Bill 74. Senate Bill 74 was another maternal health bill regarding maternal mortality review teams and the data they analyze. It also requires the Cabinet for Health and Family Services to keep track of the birth and intervention types in hospitals across Kentucky. Senate Bill 74 was signed into law by Governor Beshear on April 18th.

Another potential step forward was Senate Bill 142, a paid parental leave bill for state employees in Kentucky. No one should have to sacrifice their financial security to care for their family. Paid parental leave would allow Kentucky state employees to take the time they need to care for a new child without losing their income or savings. Black mothers are more likely than white mothers to be primary or co-breadwinners for their families, but less likely to have access to paid leave. Paid parental leave would help address the racial wealth gap and boost economic security for Black and Brown families. Senate Bill 142 passed out of the Senate, but stalled in the House. We will continue advocating for paid family leave in 2025.

Historically in Kentucky, the fight for reproductive rights excluded Black and Brown Kentuckians who did not have the same limited rights and already narrow access to reproductive health as their white counterparts. The Dobbs v. Jackson's Women's Health Organization decision, which overturned Roe V. Wade, forever changed the nature of our abortion access work in Kentucky. Abortion remains inaccessible under almost all circumstances. The ACLU-KY's Reproductive Freedom Project has fought for the right of pregnant Kentuckians to decide, for themselves, if and when to start a family. While we saw inaction by our elected officials during session, we will continue our work in harm reduction until comprehensive health care access is accessible to all Kentuckians.

HOUSE BILL 5 & THE IMPACT ON BLACK LOUISVILLE

Kentucky's carceral system is in desperate need of reform. In Louisville, it's an ongoing concern with an outsized impact on Black populations. House Bill 5, dubbed by the Kentucky Center for Economic Policy (KyPolicy) as, "the most sweeping expansion of the state's criminal statutes in decades,"[7] was previewed in September 2023 and quickly made its way past committee and the full House in the first half of session. This bill was met with robust opposition for its increase in incarceration, the risk of increased fatal overdoses, and its cruelty to unhoused Kentuckians. House Bill 5 pushes limited funds away from investments in education and healthcare and toward increased incarceration. According to KyPolicy, HB 5 will cost Kentuckians nearly $1 billion dollars over the next decade.[8] This bill will disproportionately harm Black and Brown Kentuckians who continue to be overrepresented in criminal justice spaces.[9]

We see the harm caused by incarceration all across our country, including Kentucky. In the upcoming 2025 legislative session, we hope to address some of these harms through proactive legislation designed to support families harmed by incarceration.[10] We are working now to craft legislation that would make a persons' status as a primary caretaker a mitigating factor during sentencing. Kentucky has the second highest rate of children with incarcerated parents in the nation. The Annie E. Casey Foundation reports 12% of Kentucky kids have had a parent who has experienced incarceration. This deeply impacts a child's formative years, and it's included as a question in the Adverse Childhood Experiences (ACE) screening tool. The questionnaire is designed to measure trauma's impact on health. Outside of the relationship between a high ACE score and negative health outcomes (both physical and mental), study after study demonstrates the severe negative effects of an incarcerated parent on a child.[11]

According to the Bureau of Justice Statistics, in 2016, 47% of individuals in state prisons and 57% in federal prisons were parents of minor children.[12] This indicates that nearly half of all incarcerated individuals nationwide are parents to minor children. The proportions are higher when it comes to Kentucky, with 64% of women and 55% of men incarcerated by the state

KYPOLICY, HB 5

WILL COST KENTUCKIANS NEARLY $1 BILLION DOLLARS OVER THE NEXT DECADE. THIS BILL WILL DISPROPORTIONATELY HARM BLACK AND BROWN KENTUCKIANS WHO CONTINUE TO BE OVERREPRESENTED IN CRIMINAL JUSTICE SPACES.

are parents.[13] Children of women who are incarcerated are five times more likely to end up in foster care than children of men who are incarcerated. Further, women who are primary caretakers and are incarcerated also have their parental rights taken away most often. These numbers are especially concerning given that moms are more likely to be primary caregivers to children and Kentucky incarcerates women at some of the highest rates in the nation.[14]

The state of Black Louisville is intrinsically linked to how lawmakers — both state and local — choose to invest funds and craft legislation. Our elected officials speak volumes with their actions, and we must hold them accountable. If lawmakers are not representing our interests, we must use our power, our voice, and our vote to elect those who will.

WHEN INJUSTICE BECOMES LAW, REBELLION BECOMES DUTY: HOW COALITION BUILDING IS NECESSARY TO SUSTAIN OUR COMMONWEALTH

KAILA ADIA STORY, PH.D.
Audre Lorde Endowed Chair in Race, Gender, Class & Sexuality Studies Women's & Gender Studies and Pan African Studies University of Louisville

We are at war. A war over ideas, critical academic theories, and who gets to feel they belong in our city, our state, and our country. During this 2024 legislative session, Republicans in Kentucky decided to attack diversity, equity, and inclusion (DEI), gender-affirming care, books, and school curriculum that reflects any form of diversity. They planned to use our tax dollars to create policy that endangered and left out so many constituents.

Black LGBTQ+ constituents in Louisville and in our state will suffer, die, and live in despair if new bills are proposed in the 2025 legislative session under these bills. Make no mistake, Republicans are invested in doing this because they have witnessed the power that is held within Louisville's Black LGBTQ+ communities. Republicans understand that the biggest threat to their anti-Black and anti-Queer agendas are diverse, equitable, and inclusive education, gender-affirming care, affordable housing, and the freedom to live unburdened by the harmful systems of racial biases and gendered and sexual animus.

During the 2024 legislative session, Republicans introduced three anti-DEI bills and 14 anti-LGBTQ+ bills.[1] More specifically, Senate Bills 6 and 93 and House Bill 9 sought to remove any training or educational programs that cover "evidence-based viewpoints such as anti-racist or LGBTQ+-affirming policies".[2] Louisville Public Media also noted that the language that is used in Senate Bill 6 directly reflects the sentiment found in former U.S. President Donald Trump's federal attempts at attacking DEI programming when he was in the White House.[3] Of the 14 anti-LGBTQ+ bills, House Bill 47, aimed at undoing the Fairness Ordinance, is one of the most drastic.[4] The Fairness Ordinance, which passed in Louisville in 1999 and is now in place in 24 counties in Kentucky, protects LGBTQ+ constituents from discrimination in employment, housing, and public accommodations. If this bill is passed, it will allow Kentuckians to wield their anti-LGBTQ+ hatred at our community members, all under the guise of religious freedom.[5]

These 2024 bills were not in the interest of Kentuckians, nor did they attempt to improve or enrich our quality of life. They, in fact, intended to do the opposite. They were all meant to tell our kids and our communities that they do not belong here, nor do they deserve to thrive here. These bills don't clean up our streets, repair our roads, beautify our neighborhoods, or help anybody make their rent. Although none of these bills passed, the sentiment behind them still stands, and I guarantee that the 2025 legislative session will introduce even more harmful bills. Bills that will divide our communities, alienate our constituents, and dehumanize our children. They are a profound waste of our city's and state's time and money. They are meant and designed to distract folks from their bread-and-butter needs. Generational poverty, equitable access to education, and the benefits of growing up and living in safe neighborhoods need to be addressed by our legislators. Republicans are lying to constituents. Outlawing Black LGBTQ+ identities and banning Black and Queer curricula and books won't help anyone in our state.

The time is now for coalition building on behalf of the groups that are consistently being told by our legislators that they don't belong because they're Black or because they're LGBTQIA+ or because they're both. We need to let our legislators know once and for all that anti-Black and anti-Queer discrimination in the form of public policy and law will not be tolerated in our communities, cities, or state. Coalitions are a threat to harmful systems and our Kentucky legislature is just that, a harmful system that seeks to divide communities and to stifle and suffocate all of the inclusive and historical gains our communities have worked so tirelessly to set in place. They are coming for us, all of us, and all of us have a duty to respond individually and collectively. All of us or none of us! In Solidarity!

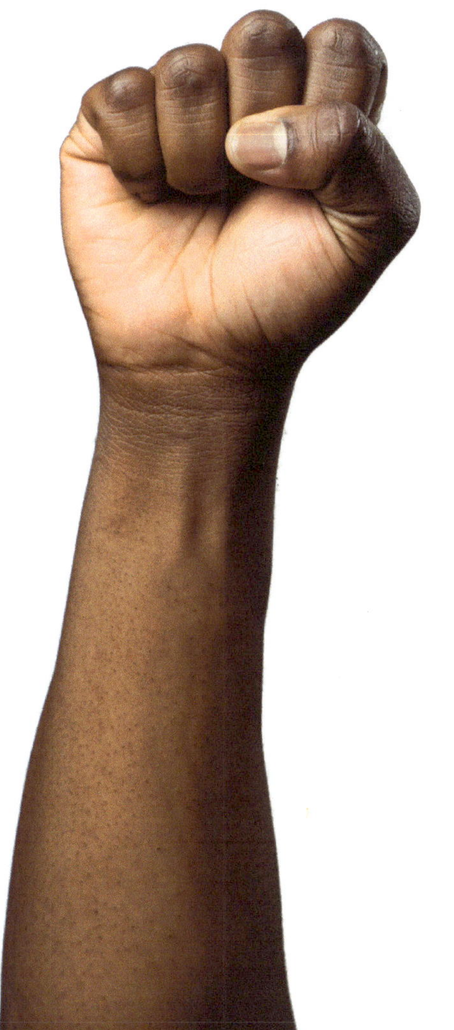

KEY TAKEAWAYS FROM THE HISTORY OF POLICING IN LOUISVILLE: A FACT-FINDING REPORT ON INSTITUTIONAL HARMS

REPORT BY: FELICIA JAMISON, PH.D.; SIDDHANT ISSAR, PH.D.; AND CATHERINE FOSL, PH.D., WITH MYA TODD, ETHAN GORTON, AND ISABELLA JOHNSON

KEY TAKEAWAYS BY: CATHERINE FOSL, PH.D., AND CHERIE DAWSON-EDWARDS, PH.D.

This 2024 history report began as one part of Louisville Metro Government's multi-part community repair project, **Truth & Transformation Initiative (TTI),** which started in the wake of Breonna Taylor's murder and the racial justice reckonings of 2020. The Greenberg Administration discontinued the remainder of the TTI while the research for these findings was underway.

Completed by two historians, a political scientist, and a team of University of Louisville student assistants, this study outlines how police practices and policies have disproportionately affected Blacks and other people of color, tracing historical patterns from the late 18th century to the present. The history report forms a counterpart to the 2023 U.S. Department of Justice (DOJ) report, but one that looks at centuries rather than simply one decade.

Institutional harm was defined as patterns of negative and detrimental effects over time that are specific to certain groups, and exist on a continuum ranging from discourteous treatment to greater surveillance all the way to violent beatings and the brutal taking of innocent lives.

Sources used include early court records, police bulletins, daily and weekly newspapers, existing interviews, and organizational newsletters, as well as previously published works on the topic.

THEMES FROM THE RESEARCH

Across the history of policing in Louisville, three themes stood out:

1. Patterns of racial discrimination that were frequent, ongoing, consistent, and set the stage for unequal treatment of other groups

2. Lack of adequate internal accountability in Louisville's police force

3. Persistent hostility and opposition within the force to forms of external oversight (a dynamic that worsened as technology modernized)

ORIGINS OF POLICING IN LOUISVILLE

The first local police, known as "watchmen," formed in 1806 to protect early white colonists from indigenous people. These were not slave patrols, but they shared the same purpose — maintaining order based on racial hierarchies that considered enslaved persons as property and treated all Blacks and people of color as inferior. Over time, these practices evolved into more structured law enforcement that very intentionally left racial inequities intact.

INSTITUTIONAL RACISM AND DISCRIMINATORY PRACTICES

From disproportionate arrests in Black communities in the 19th and 20th centuries to upholding segregation in housing and public spaces until the 1960s, law enforcement has played a major role in maintaining racial and social inequalities. Black Louisvillians routinely faced harsher penalties and were targeted disproportionately in comparison to whites. A few 20th century examples include:

- **On the very same day the U.S. Supreme Court declared Louisville's housing segregation ordinance unconstitutional in 1917, a local Black teenaged girl was beaten by police right outside her front door for refusing to answer questions about a neighbor.**

- **In the 1950s, the still-all-white Jefferson County police failed to protect Andrew Wade's family from racist violence in Shively, and the Wade home was dynamited by arsonists in June 1954 despite 24-hour police protection.**

Inside the police force, although Louisville hired its first Black officer in 1922, it took more than four decades for Black and white officers to be allowed even to ride in the same car (1965). Only multiple lawsuits filed by determined minority officers (led by Shelby Lanier, Jr.) brought about widespread hiring or promotion of Black or women police officers.

POLICE BRUTALITY AND COMMUNITY PROTESTS

Across the 20th century, police brutality remained a reality for Black Louisvillians, but Black-led organizations fought against police violence and for fair treatment. High-profile incidents, such as the May 1968 Parkland uprising following police mistreatment of a Black community leader, underscore the long-standing tensions between the police and marginalized communities.

Even the passage of equal rights laws in the 1960s did not end police brutality directed to Black, Indigenous, and People of Color (BIPOC) communities. Soon after, economic changes such as deindustrialization caused the loss of good-paying jobs, and a new public opposition to government assistance programs prompted a resurgence of the Ku Klux Klan. When the Marshall family desegregated a Pleasure Ridge Park neighborhood in 1985, for example, investigation of the arson fire that soon destroyed their home revealed a KKK unit composed of local police and called Confederate Order of Patriots (COPS). The unit was disbanded, but not all of the officers were fired.

At the turn of the 21st century, police killings of at least six Black men in rapid succession between 1999-2002 (Desmond Rudolph, Rodney Abernathy, Clifford Lewis, Antwan Bryant, Marshall Marby, and James Taylor) — most of whom were unarmed and none of whom had a gun — caused community outrage and mistrust to soar. An earlier high-profile death happened in 1998 when Adrian Reynolds was found dead in a jail cell while at the Jefferson County Jail. Yet, no meaningful accountability measures resulted. The report documents persisting 21st century institutional harms directed at Black and other marginalized communities that paved a clear path to Breonna Taylor's violent death at the hands of Louisville Metro Police Department (LMPD) in 2020.

LACK OF ACCOUNTABILITY AND PERSISTENT INEQUALITY

The report sheds light on systemic failures to hold police officers accountable for racial violence. Despite numerous complaints and documented instances of brutality, the police have fiercely resisted significant reforms. Attempts to establish civilian oversight, such as an effective Civilian Police Review Board, starting in the 1960s, triggered mass protests from police unions, halting the measure and increasing community mistrust.

RECENT DEVELOPMENTS AND THE NEED FOR REFORM

This history report provides further context and evidence for the findings of the DOJ investigation (2016-2021) into the Louisville Metro Police Department (LMPD). Both have revealed ongoing patterns of discrimination, excessive use of force, and unconstitutional practices. These findings reflect the historical continuity of institutional harms, signaling an urgent need for systemic reform to create public trust and protect the rights of all residents.

Key Recommendations From the Report Include:

1. **Police Accountability:** The report emphasizes the need for external

democratic mechanisms for accountability and transparency in order to build trust between the police and marginalized communities. Citizens, especially those most affected, should have a direct role in overseeing
police actions.

2. **Residential Requirements for Officers:** One concrete suggestion is to reintroduce a residential rewquirement for a portion of the police force. This was an early policy in pre-Civil War Louisville, ensuring that officers were invested in the communities they served.

3. **Structural Reform and Investment in Social Services:** The report calls for a shift in resources from policing to social services, public programs, and economic safety nets to address social, economic, and mental health issues comprehensively, rather than using police as the primary institution to manage these societal challenges.

4. **Restorative Justice and Compensation:** The report advocates for a process of amends, possibly including monetary compensation, for victims of police abuse and their communities — particularly those who have suffered intergenerational harm. [Louisville Metro has often outspent neighboring cities in settling civil suits resulting from the mistreatments described here.]

5. **Implementation of DOJ Recommendations:** The report insists that the DOJ's findings must be considered within the broader historical context of policing in Louisville to create meaningful, lasting change.

Scan QR Code to access "The History of Policing in Louisville: A Fact-Finding Report on Institutional Harms"

THE STATE OF WHITE ALLYSHIP IN BLACK LOUISVILLE

CHRISTINA SHADLE
Chief of Staff, Amped

History is threatening to repeat itself in Louisville.

A synopsis of Dr. George C. Wright's book, "Life Behind a Veil", defines the period between the Civil War and the Great Depression in Louisville as one marked by "polite racism."[1] While "Louisville blacks escaped the harsh violence that was a fact of life for blacks in the Deep South" and "consistently enjoyed and exercised an oft-contested but never effectively retracted enfranchisement," it was true then, as one can argue now, that their votes were overridden by "a substantial paternalism carried over from antebellum days in Louisville." According to Wright, whites routinely "salved their [consciences] without really threatening an established order. And blacks, obliged to be grateful for the assistance, generally refrained from arguing for real social and political equality for fear of jeopardizing a partially improved situation and regressing to a status similar to that of other southern blacks."[2]

As a white person, my particular concern is for my present-day white counterparts as we teeter between real, substantive change and merely assuaging our consciences. Although we have more than a century of muscle memory around lending support for a "limited uplifting of blacks in society," I want to believe that white Louisville is capable of more.

I want to believe that white Louisville is moved by the numbers: that homeownership is nearly twice as high among whites as compared to Blacks;[3] that white students are twice as likely to have a bachelor's degree than Black students;[4] that Black workers in Louisville make less in every single industry than do their white counterparts; that life expectancy is now a full 15 years less in the predominantly Black West End as compared to the overwhelmingly white eastern parts of the county.

I want to believe that we know these numbers and that, in knowing them, we are disturbed by them.

I recognize every person can't take on every element of the fight against inequity. But we can, and we should, take on the fight in our particular lanes. As a matter of professional responsibility, I expect white bankers to understand the racial wealth gap and the undercapitalization that Black businesses face.[5] I expect white realtors to understand redlining and the artificially low appraisal rates in Black neighborhoods that result from it.[6] I believe lawyers should understand racial disparities in sentencing and imprisonment Black children excel in environments with teachers who look like them.[7][8] When I say "understand," I mean lawyers should have studied these issues, paid careful attention to how they manifest in their work, talked with people about them — white and Black — and then worked to find ways to disrupt these patterns. This can mean doing your own work differently and, very often, it means supporting the systems-change work of others — especially that of Black Louisville.

There are capable, courageous, unflinching Black leaders working every day to advance programs and policies that have the power to change this city. White Louisville, they have done the work for us! All we are asked to do is follow their blueprint, their Path Forward.[9] Engage in the ways they are asking of us. Show up. Invest money freely. Stand with them when times are relatively easy, and stand in front of them when they are fired upon. Take a hit. At least once, be the one to stand for something and let it sting. Odds are, as white people, we'll end up just fine.

Louisville's racial problems are deep and entrenched. Yet, they are not inevitable, and they are not unsolvable. Our history of polite racism need not define our future. White allies, we must not be the people who momentarily marched in the streets only to retreat from the fight in the boardroom, or at the closing table, in the courtroom or in the classroom. Our Black brothers and sisters deserve more, and we are capable of more. I sincerely want to believe that. Let's work together to make it so.

"I EXPECT WHITE BANKERS TO UNDERSTAND THE RACIAL WEALTH GAP AND THE UNDERCAPITALIZATION THAT BLACK BUSINESSES FACE.

I EXPECT WHITE REALTORS TO UNDERSTAND REDLINING AND THE ARTIFICIALLY LOW APPRAISAL RATES IN BLACK NEIGHBORHOODS THAT RESULT FROM IT.

I BELIEVE LAWYERS SHOULD UNDERSTAND RACIAL DISPARITIES IN SENTENCING AND IMPRISONMENT JUST AS EDUCATORS SHOULD UNDERSTAND THAT BLACK CHILDREN EXCEL IN ENVIRONMENTS WITH TEACHERS WHO LOOK LIKE THEM."

THE LOUISVILLE METRO POLICE DEPARTMENT MUST DO BETTER FOR BLACK PEOPLE

SHAMEKA PARRISH-WRIGHT,
District 3 Louisville Metro Council Chairwoman, Executive Director for VOCAL-KY

Let's be clear that the state of Black Louisville differs based on the Black person you ask. Just like my mama, aunts, and uncles have said, "Many Black people feel all they have to do is stay Black and die."

People like me have chosen social justice as a pathway to true freedom. Many African Americans consider themselves working class, using their education and skills to improve their lives and the lives of those they love. Nutrition, housing, healthcare, transportation, and some luxuries are things we all deserve. We as Black Louisvillians want to access all of these resources in the safest way possible. Unfortunately, more often than not, policing has not contributed to Black Louisvillians' ability to survive and thrive. In fact, it has hampered it. The Louisville Metro Police Department (LMPD) is an overwhelmingly racist and problematic institution. Report after report, including from the U.S. Department of Justice[1] and the University of Louisville[2]— details years-long violence and discrimination against Black people.

This is not the opinion of an activist. It is factual information. Unfortunately, racist police institutions are worldwide. Anti-Blackness is the United States' most plentiful export. Louisville is one of many labs for the tools of anti-Blackness and racism through policing. I do not say this to impugn the character of any currently serving officer, or to question their motives or morals. I know many police officers who want to serve their community, and some of whom are themselves Black. At one point, because of the Drug Abuse Resistance Education (D.A.R.E.) program, I wanted to be a police officer. I wanted to make a difference in my community. What I am emphasizing is the problematic nature of policing, because it needs to be said constantly (this was especially apparent during the civil unrest in the justice for[3] Breonna Taylor movement, as illustrated by this report.)

It is critically important that Black Louisvillians connect their struggles with the struggles of Black communities the world over. In my role as the Executive Director of VOCAL-KY, we hosted Ali Bantu Ashanti, an Afro-Colombian civil rights lawyer. He spoke of the military police wantonly executing Black people and that police do not face any consequences for these killings. It was astonishing how eerily similar Colombia's policing practices are to Louisville's. Colombia is far from the only country in the world that violently polices Black communities.

As someone who has long advocated for police reform, and now as a sitting Louisville Metro Councilwoman, I must reiterate the importance of placing the LMPD under a consent decree. More information on the consent decree and its process can be found here. [4]

What many in Black Louisville want is a basic foundation for community oversight of police. While a consent decree will not overturn the baked-in racism of policing, it will at least put more checks on use of force, hiring practices, and protocols. As a Louisville Metro Councilwoman, I worked to submit a resolution to adopt the Peoples' Consent Decree. [5] I am hopeful this will send a message that Louisville Metro Government is not just a rubber stamp to the LMPD, and to let the LMPD know it must start doing better.

We also must acknowledge that Black Louisvillians are not monolithic, and some Black Louisvillians do not experience the LMPD as a barrier to their life, liberty, and pursuit of happiness. However, part of the resolution I introduced and read into record for Louisville Metro Council on June 6th includes the reallocation of surplus public monies away from the LMPD. Those monies would go towards more, and better, public services like housing, healthcare, and neighborhood investment. What if, instead of funding additional police overtime, Louisville Metro Government invested even more in Black-owned businesses and startups? Or made homeownership more accessible? The quality of life for Black Louisvillians would be uplifted if public funding was diverted away from policing and surveillance and invested in small businesses and entrepreneurs, and direct services. More broadly, what would Black Louisville look like if we reimagined our public safety, and incentivized the aunties, uncles, and faith leaders already engaged in conflict resolution in our neighborhoods? How do we uplift small, start-up, anti-violence advocates trying to make a difference who aren't given opportunities to connect to funding because they might lack "administrative capacity" or the "ability to scale"?

For me, the task before us is simple. We can address the LMPD's patterns and practices of discrimination against Black Louisvillians and uplift the success of Black Louisvillians by limiting funding of the LMPD and investing in our Black neighbors. How do we do this? We must organize with each other across lines of class, gender, and political leaning. We must recognize our collective power, take direct action, and train up our young Black leaders so that when we all become elders, the next generation is properly educated to carry the torch. Here, at VOCAL-KY, we prioritize training directly impacting people to be leaders so they can be the decision makers about policies that will touch their lives. Learn more at VOCAL-KY.ORG.

****TRIGGER WARNING

WHAT HAPPENS?

SADIQA N. REYNOLDS, ESQ.
President Emeritus, Louisville Urban League
CEO Perception Institute

On August 26, 2024, a federal judge dismissed felony deprivation of rights under the color of law charges against officers in the Breonna Taylor case. In effect, ruling that police were not responsible for the death of Breoona Taylor and instead blaming her boyfriend, Kenneth Walker. We learned this past Friday that prosecutors intend to appeal that ruling and so the case is now heading to the Sixth Circuit Court of Appeals.

We mourn for the life of Breonna Taylor. We grieve for her mother and sister and all that they lost. If we mention Kenneth Walker at all, we talk about him losing the love of his life, his future forever changed. We do not treat him as the surviving victim of the terror he and Breonna were subjected to in the wee hours of March 13, 2020 in Louisville, Kentucky. We lost Breonna Taylor but walked away from Kenneth.

Imagine taking your girlfriend out for dinner, then coming home, watching a movie, and falling asleep on the couch, only to be awakened by the sound of unidentified intruders breaking through the door of that home. Kenneth fired his weapon. He had a right to do so. In Kentucky, we have a right to defend our property and ourselves. He didn't stand his ground in the way that George Zimmerman claimed to have stood his when he killed Trayvon Martin. Breonna and Kenny were not the aggressors. They had no place to retreat, nowhere to run, nowhere to hide. As the door was busted open, Kenny fired a gun licensed to him. Police returned fire and, in seconds, Breonna was dead.

All neighbors, save one who changed his story, said police did not announce themselves. The neighbors' memories seem consistent with Kenny's behavior because when he could get to a phone, he called the police. He dialed 911 and pleaded for help. We listened to the call and became witnesses to the sounds of his terror. We have seen the video now. We know he was pushed from the home at gunpoint and threatened with dogs. The video captured outside the apartment is reminiscent of slave catchers siccing dogs on runaways, or those marching toward freedom.

This is not an attempt to portray Kenneth as a freedom fighter. We don't need him to be an angel. We need him to be acknowledged as a man. We are recognizing his dignity. We are acknowledging his humanity. Something the police and the system have refused to do. In fact, not only did Kenneth have to watch Breonna die, but he was denied the right to grieve her death. They refused to allow him to attend her funeral. He listened instead over the phone. He heard the cries and screams at the funeral through a phone. Perhaps he heard the casket close. He hasn't said. He was not there to comfort her mother or his own. And no one was there to comfort him.

Breonna was the love of his life. They shot her to death and threatened to turn dogs on him.

Then they not only encouraged a narrative that demonized him; they sued him.

We know now that the warrant used to authorize a SWAT team to enter her home was falsified and, still, a federal court judge has ruled that police were not at fault for her death. They blame Kenny– the surviving victim.

Kenny's story illustrates the brutality Black people have been subjected to by systems that work aggressively to put and keep us in our place, then offer nothing to help us heal from the trauma they've caused. There is a need to address the emotion evoked in Black bystanders forced to watch as those who look like us are viciously and mercilessly extinguished under circumstances that white people survive.

What happens when the government kills your girlfriend? Do you have to go in and pack your own things in the house where she lost her life, or do they send someone for you? Does the government provide mental health counseling or do you pay out of pocket? When dogs are sicced on you, are you forever triggered by barking? Who lowers the flag for Kenny?

Kenny Walker belonged in that apartment that night. Police did not. He was not responsible for Breonna's death. Black people have never been positioned to save those we love from those who would kill us, rape us, or torture us. I don't know what the rest of the country remembers, but I know that many of us living in Louisville will never forget the day we first heard Kenny's call to 911 or what it felt like to finally watch the videos that police said did not exist.

He was not her killer. He was her lover. The last smile she shared was for him. The last hug she had was his. He was her last kiss. Her last moments on earth will forever mark a before and after for him. He has to live with that.

What does a community offer a man robbed of his dignity? How far can you push pain down, and where does it go? These are things I have wondered since I met Kenny. These are questions I consider in quiet moments when I remember his eyes and what he looks like when he thinks no one is watching.

Honestly, I saw a similar cloud in the eyes of Darnella Frazier when I met the young woman who was only a teen when she filmed George Floyd's death. There is a lifetime of trauma wrapped in witnessing the moments of watching a life end at the hands of people paid to protect. What is it like to film a murder? Do you feel weak or strong? Do you feel anything at all? When Darnella Frazier spoke of the death threats that forced her and her mother from their home, I wondered if the government that killed George Floyd was also responsible for her healing, or at a minimum, her moving expenses.

Darnella Frazier was a victim. Kenneth Walker was a victim. The fact that we were pushed to protest in a pandemic in order to declare their humanity and ours was inhumane. We just keep pushing down the pain. Nothing is the same and not enough has changed.

EDUCATION

"

AT THE CORE OF THE EDUCATIONAL IN AMERICA IS THE LIE THAT SCHOOL WAS DESIGNED FOR BLACK MINDS.

"

JOHN DAVID MARSHALL, ED.D.

FUTURE FOCUS OF RACIAL EQUITY

BJ BUNTON
Executive Administrator
Diversity, Equity, and Poverty Department
Jefferson County Public Schools

Jefferson County Public Schools (JCPS) is entering its seventh year with a Racial Equity Policy.[1] JCPS is one of a handful of districts that has an equity policy with a specific focus on race, which is profound. Let's be clear: A policy alone is meaningless without an enacted plan with tangible goals, actions, and protocols to monitor the change of outcomes. A policy is meaningless without a school system and community supporting it.

The initial plan that was developed to address the Racial Equity Policy's tenets and dictates included 22 metrics and 96 strategies, which was rather convoluted, lacking clear goals and progress monitoring aligned to the dictates of the policy. It was a good starting point but, to bring about the change necessary, there was a need for a shift in the plan in order to become more targeted and focused. In January 2023, JCPS began work to revamp the initial plan in the form of a logic model (JCPS will soon publish a website that will outline the plan described, including the goals and measures). The logic model that has been developed narrows the scope and focus of the work in our district as it relates to racial equity. In this model, there are clear inputs, outputs, outcomes with targeted measures, and goals aligned with outcomes.

The long-term outcome (impact) that JCPS seeks to achieve through the Racial Equity Policy plan is racial educational equity for all students, as measured through student enrollment and academic data. Included in this revamped plan are two tertiary (midterm) outcomes:

1. **Promote the success of all students** through the minimization of gaps among students of color and white students, while raising achievement for all. In addition, improve culture and climate in schools and central office by providing ongoing technical, pedagogical, social-emotional, and curriculum training and support.

2. **Eliminate institutional and structural policy and practices that perpetuate inequities and create systemic racial disparities in educational opportunities and outcomes.** This will be done through the review/altering of policies and practices in schools and central office through the use of the Racial Equity Analysis Protocol (REAP). In addition, increase the diversity of school and district staff to more closely reflect the demographic of the district's student population.

The long-term and mid-term outcomes are undergirded by five, data-driven goals that are connected directly to the Racial Equity Policy tenets. These will support JCPS in determining progress toward reaching the desired outcomes for all students, particularly students of color:

1. Accelerate the percentage of students of color who are **Proficient/Distinguished on state testing** in reading and math (measured by district, state, and national assessment data).

2. Increase in percentage of students of color reporting **sense of belonging** (measured by district and state survey data).

3. Increase in **postsecondary readiness** for students of color (measured by district and state data and benchmarks).

4. Increase in percentage of **teachers** of color, **administrators** of color, and **retention** of teachers of color (measured by district demographic data).

5. Increase in percentage of total policies and practices determined to move forward with no changes (measure: REAP dashboard).

The revamping of the plan called for each central office department to not only examine the activities that are done to support the broad demographic of students in JCPS, but to really narrow the scope of what is being done and its impact or lack thereof on outcomes for students of color. This was achieved by having each department examine their activities through a list of qualifying questions, resulting in supporting and directing activities that align with the determined Racial Equity Plan outcomes. In addition, each department had to determine how they would measure progress for each of those supporting activities. With this plan comes monitoring and oversight. Bimonthly, representatives from each central office department meet to talk through progress being made with those activities and the goals that have been established in the plan.

It is my belief that we are on the right track with the development of a plan and protocol utilizing a logic model. I am confident that we will continue to see changed outcomes for all students, particularly for our students of color. As a district, we will continue to revisit and revamp what is in place to ensure continued growth and that JCPS is on track to meet/exceed the outcomes established. This will allow for a manner of transparency and accountability internally and externally. We need the community's support and involvement not only through accountability, but also through engagement with and advocacy for the Racial Equity Policy and its subsequent plan.

> “A POLICY ALONE IS MEANINGLESS WITHOUT AN ENACTED PLAN WITH TANGIBLE GOALS, ACTIONS, AND PROTOCOLS TO MONITOR THE CHANGE OF OUTCOMES.
>
> A POLICY IS MEANINGLESS WITHOUT A SCHOOL SYSTEM AND COMMUNITY SUPPORTING IT.”

HBCUS ARE IMPERATIVE TO BLACK PROGRESS; THEY NEED FINANCIAL SUPPORT FROM LIBERAL ALLIES

DR. KEVIN COSBY
President, Simmons College

Presidents of Historically Black Colleges and Universities (HBCUs) have always known that our institutional success depends far less on our allies' exercises in antiracist rhetoric and much more on their exercises in antiracist resource sharing.

Benjamin Elijah Mays, a man I count among my heroes and a former president of one of America's most prestigious HBCUs, Morehouse College, understood this distinction quite well. At the college's Centennial Commencement Convocation, he issued this warning:

"Discrimination in the future will not be administered by poor whites and the people who believe in segregation, but by the liberals who believe in a desegregated society…who will wine and dine with us in the swankiest hotels, work with us, and still discriminate against us when it comes to money and power."[1]

Nearly 60 years later, Mays's words weigh heavy on my mind. While the house of white supremacy may have had its foundation laid and its framing put up by openly racist hands, it is the liberals today who are not so much helping to tear down that house (as they might imagine), but who are often, instead, busily hanging the drywall and putting on the finishing touches.

I have come to accept the permanence, to some degree or another, of that house here in America. At the same time, I know that our efforts to oppose its permanent influence over Black people's ability to self-determine must always endure. History shows us that when it comes to breaking that stranglehold over our genuine autonomy, we are never in a greater position to do so than when our Black institutions are well capitalized.

Given the significant role that philanthropy has always played in our institutional capacity to serve and uplift the community, the cold indifference that has broadly characterized the donor class' attitudes toward our Black institutions over the past twenty years suggests that the future described by Mays has indeed arrived.

A report released last month noted how, from 2002 to 2019, foundational support for HBCUs fell 30% from $65 million to $45 million.[2] During 2015-2019, the nation's eight Ivy League schools received a combined $5.5 billion in philanthropic dollars while, in that same period of time, the entirety of the nation's 100 HBCUs received only $303 million. To look at the average Ivy League school and the foundation funding it receives is to see an amount 178 times greater than that received by the average HBCU.[3] Harvard University, for instance, boasts an endowment of $53 billion; the value of all HBCU endowments taken together is less than 10% of that.[45] And so, as the endowments of non-HBCUs continue to accumulate with charitable giving reaching its highest levels historically, HBCUs keep rattling their tin to an indifferent philanthropic sector.

What this tells me is that there is a definite disconnect between our liberal and progressive allies' stated support for the cause of Black uplift and their commitment of resources toward that end. After all, when it comes to Black people maximizing their potential, there is only one group of institutions established for that express purpose. There is only one group of institutions with a definite, proven track record of fulfilling that mission: Black institutions. While only constituting a mere 3% of our nation's colleges, our HBCUs punch well above their weight in their development of America's Black professional class. They disproportionately produce the number of Black engineers (40%), Black doctors and dentists (70%), Black judges (80%), and Black public school teachers (50%).[6] It is that last statistic, in particular, that — when I think of the current state of Black Louisville and what's needed to guarantee an elevating effect on the community — points to the absolutely critical role of those institutions.

Consider the following: When low-income Black students have at least one Black

teacher in the 3rd, 4th, or 5th grade, they are nearly 40% less likely to drop out of school.[78] Here in Jefferson County, we are a majority-minority school system that has long suffered from persistent gaps in graduation rates between its white and Black students. Given how the district's Black student population (37%) is nearly three and a half times the total number of its Black teachers (11%), how can we possibly wonder why our Black youth are significantly less likely to see a commencement ceremony than their white peers? Worse yet, how can we not possibly realize that we already have the exact means to treat and fix that problem? We know that the solution lies in our HBCUs. The data tells us that it is those institutions that are overwhelmingly preparing Black teachers to be in those public school classrooms where they can model success for Black children, steer them away from self-doubt and directionlessness, and keep them on a path toward positive outcomes.

This path leads me to the issue of some much-needed honesty from our liberal and progressive allies, particularly those within the donor community whose selection of charitable causes is informed by the data. After all, if these donors' philanthropic giving is honestly guided by the data, and they want to help uplift and support the Black community, then they must necessarily invest their money into HBCUs. It is past time to end the legacy of neglect. In the fight for racial justice, continuing to overlook or ignore how singularly vital these institutions are in conditioning success for Black people is to keep a thumb on the scale for white supremacy.

Regrettably, Mays' prediction about soft discrimination by liberals has, indeed, become our greatest obstacle today. However, I have seen firsthand the possibility of radical change when liberals and progressives embrace an institutional vision of authentic Black empowerment — one in which the control, culture, and concerns of the institution are necessarily and straightforwardly Black. Simmons College of Kentucky — the nation's most recently designated HBCU where I have proudly served as president for 20 years — is one such example. Over the last decade, we have become a major economic driver for Louisville, generating a nearly $51 million financial effect in the city and beyond. As a provider of the kind of unique educational experience that Black high school graduates are seeking, we are helping counter our city's population decrease by attracting students from 28 different states as well as bringing in scholars and academics whose skill sets will, in turn, help expand the Black professional class here in Louisville. Additionally, our operating budget continues to grow. It has increased nearly 8,000% since 2005, to $16,000,000, now ranking as the largest of any Black institution in the state of Kentucky. Because of that, we will be able to keep making the kinds of capital investments in the community that redound to the benefit of not just Black Louisville, but Louisville as a whole.

I list these accomplishments because there is a direct link between Simmons' ability to provide this increasing level of service to the community and the great civic-mindedness of local donors like the late

David A. Jones Sr. and organizations like the Gheens and James Graham Brown Foundation. They believed in us at a time when it was unpopular to do so; when the local philanthropic network was casting aspersions on our relevancy, predicting failure, and even preparing a feasibility study to discourage donors from giving their money to an unapologetically Black institution. Before the ink had dried on that study, though, we had proven them wrong. It was because those aforementioned individuals had listened with courageous ears to the case for HBCUs. Without perhaps ever hearing the words of Benjamin Mays, they nonetheless understood the imperative in his dictum that, "The abolition of economic, political, and philanthropic discrimination is the first order of the day, not for the good of Negroes alone, but for the nation as a whole."[9] Today, I am calling on more mavericks from the philanthropic community to similarly heed that exhortation to radical altruism, and to be the friend that Black people so desperately need right now.

BAD MAGIC
McMann
UNWANTEDS
ISLAND OF LEGENDS
DARKSTALKER
RICK RIORDAN'S

BLACK STUDENTS CAN AND WILL LEARN AT GRACE JAMES AND DUBOIS ACADEMIES

BLACK GIRLS CAN LEARN

DR. LATONYA FRAZIER
Principal of Grace James Academy

Grace James Academy of Excellence was established in 2020 to eliminate the pushout educational experience that many Black/Brown girls feel as they enter the doors of mainstream institutions. We believe at Grace James Academy that through providing a strong connection to the curriculum, powerful social emotional programs, and qualified, dedicated teachers, we can eliminate the disconnect that many minority female students feel during their schooling.

Grace James is built on the foundational principles of our mission, vision, and CROWN (Collaboration, Resilience, Originality, Willingness, and Narrative) values. During the inception of the school, we meticulously selected verbs that caused us to perform actions that have not been done consistently for this population of brilliant females in traditional schooling. We stand firmly on the foundation of empowering, activating, and illuminating academic excellence. Minority female students come to us with many gifts that have been buried deep inside of them in order to fit in with the status quo that is required in most traditional educational spaces. Our job as Grace James educators is to give females a platform/space to advocate and reveal their brilliance, which happens through consistent empowerment, activation, and illumination.

Our day begins in a nontraditional advisory space known as Sister Circle. Sister Circle is a tier-one social emotional learning experience that provides students with consistent lessons around the CROWN values, executive functioning skills, and sisterhood. Each adult is responsible for approximately ten students to provide an extra layer of support for students within and beyond the Sister Circle.

In addition to Sister Circles, in order to help students reach their full potential, we center our work on four foci (Afrocentric curriculum; science, technology, engineering, the arts, and mathematics [STEAM]; gender-specific pedagogy; and rigor). Our staff is trained through a variety of professional readings and discussions with the aid of an onsite cultural humility coach to integrate our Afrocentric themes in all coursework. This integration occurs in both core and related arts classes. Students are familiar with our themes (identity, humanity, social justice and oppression, and African diaspora) and can readily speak to how these themes help them best relate to their coursework.

Grace James is a STEAM academy. We participate in the Jefferson County Public Schools (JCPS) Middle School Explore Pathways. Pathways are another way that we develop a sense of belonging amongst our Girls Exploring Math and Science (GEMS) by allowing them an opportunity to explore our three career pathways — informational business, engineering, and healthcare — prior to making a selection during their seventh-grade year. In addition to these pathways, we provide students with multiple art offerings including choir, orchestra, dance, and art. These classes are used as another avenue to give students an entryway into STEAM and our Afrocentric curriculum.

We approach gender-specific studies in a nontraditional way. Girls are not a monolith. Therefore, our goal is not to teach them traditional ways that girls should learn and behave. Instead, we concentrate our efforts on exposing females to career opportunities that have limited numbers of minority females, providing them with the communication tools to advocate and skills to develop continual learning habits through a strong sisterhood.

Teachers are given tools to ensure they are familiar with personalizing learning to provide the appropriate level of rigor. Many of our teachers have adopted a Modern Classroom approach to ensure students are able to work at their own pace with teacher-developed structures and expectations. This approach has allowed teachers to be able to seamlessly pull small groups and accelerate and intervene instantly based on formative and summative data.

Grace James Academy of Excellence is a growing school that continues to onboard new staff annually. We provide them with an intense onboarding process, which includes an assigned mentor, professional development beginning in the summer, and continual access to multiple coaches and administrators throughout their Grace James experience. It is mandatory that we onboard staff members regardless of their years of experience, as at this academy we will be unlearning understandings that we may have learned in previous settings that have been deemed not to work best for our population.

Although still a new school, we are beginning to reap the benefits of our dedicated, consistent practices. Below is a chart that shows how Grace James' African-American females compare to African American females in JCPS and the

		Grace James	JCPS	State
Reading	Grade 6	46	22	26
	Grade 7	37	19	24
	Grade 8	39	20	23
Math	Grade 6	19	9	15
	Grade 7	25	10	15
	Grade 8	29	11	15
Science	Grade 7	6	4	7
Social Studies	Grade 8	27	12	16
Writing (Editing & mechanics)	Grade 8	52	24	29
Writing (On-Demand)	Grade 8	39	15	25

Performing at or above JCPS or State Average

state. As noted, we scored above both JCPS and the state in all areas with the exception of the state science scores.

Based on these results, Grace James will continue the mission, vision, and CROWN value work that is changing the trajectory of minority female students in middle and high school. The work is not finished; we are consistently researching, reading, and collaborating together to ensure we provide our GEMS with an excellent education.

BLACK BOYS CAN LEARN

DR. MONICA HUNTER
Principal of W.E.B. DuBois Academy Middle

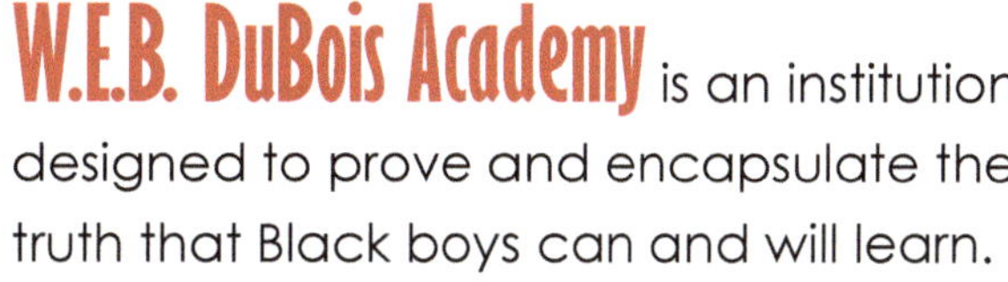

W.E.B. DuBois Academy is an institution designed to prove and encapsulate the truth that Black boys can and will learn.

Educational and systemic oppressive infrastructures in mainstream public schools are the reason there is a need for schools like DuBois. Historical constructs in America were designed with the majority of affluent males in mind. This alienates the population we serve: Black and Brown males, altogether. This pattern of oppression prevented many Black and Brown males from soaring due to the lack of relevance and rigor connected to adolescent and intellectual development and growth. Curricula, assessments, instruction, and behavioral practices were intentionally built to leave them behind. The following outlines what the leadership at W.E.B. DuBois Academy has done to prove that Black and Brown boys can and will learn.

Before one can analyze teaching and learning at an institution such as DuBois, building a culture that empowers students and staff to push themselves to excellence was necessary. Every day, students recite our school creed, which dispels the notion that our students are anything less than young men of greatness, excellence, and royalty. This is necessary because in many schools, and in society, their skin is weaponized, leading to mainstream fear and punitive outcomes, self-sabotage, or hate. Researcher Jayanti Owens, Assistant Professor of Organizational Behavior at Yale's School of Management, conducted a study connecting implicit biases to corporal and punitive consequences.[3] Unsurprisingly, she discovered that Black and Brown boys are not only punished more severely and often than their counterparts, but they are often not given a chance for true due process to take place due to the preconceived idea that the students are guilty without a chance for their voice to be heard concerning behavior or academic disparities.

Social and emotional support is the foundation of our school, but high academic standards and expectations are the walls and posts that hold our school together. Unlike many mainstream schools, W.E.B. DuBois developed a system to monitor access to grade-level instruction for all content areas throughout middle and high school. The mindsets of parents, staff, and students had to shift to that of productive struggle because the academic exposure our stakeholders had at previous schools was watered down with lower standards. These practices have made it easy for Black and Brown students to fall through the crack, widening the achievement gap.

In addition, cultural relevance is vital to reaching Black and Brown students. The teachers at DuBois Academy teach through the lens of Black and Brown people. Not only that, but a part of Afrocentricity is to understand and respect others' perspectives. Therefore, we PRIDE ourselves in teaching through mirrors and windows, which means students can see themselves throughout instruction via mirrors, but they also see and respect the experiences of others' perspectives via windows. Our teachers post learning targets, but they also explain how our PRIDE values or Afrocentric themes are relevant within each lesson that is taught.

Next, students have the opportunity to defend their learning via in-class or school-wide exhibitions. This project-based instruction aligns with student-centered learning and allows their creativity to be an intricate part of the vast educational ecosystem in which their learning is housed. Students not only show mastery of content, but they show what they know through projects, presentations, videos, art, food, etc. For an extra layer of excellence, our cafeteria or gym is turned into an exhibition space at least twice per year for students to showcase quality artifacts connected to mastery of standards. This empowers students to produce efforts of excellence and output their best work before showcasing said projects in front of community members, school staff, and parents.

Lastly, data literacy drives teaching and learning at DuBOIS Academy. The principal and assistant principals meet with their assigned departments at least once a month to unpack standards-based, grade-level assessment data and determine instructional next steps. In addition, students track their progress towards mastery after formative, summative, and district assessments. The principal and assistant principals then meet to present their department data and determine next steps for teacher feedback and coaching which, in turn, strengthens instructional practices.

These practices, along with others, have allowed us to outperform Black boys across our district and the state, and even outperform other ethnicities as recorded via state and district-based assessments. This proves that not only can Black boys learn, but they will if placed in an environment where they matter, see themselves, and are challenged to achieve academic excellence.

		DuBois	JCPS	State
Reading	Grade 6	21	22	26
	Grade 7	47	19	24
	Grade 8	39	20	23
Math	Grade 10	23	24	25
	Grade 6	13	9	15
	Grade 7	15	10	15
	Grade 8	9	11	15
	Grade 10	10	13	15
Science	Grade 7	6	4	7
Social Studies	Grade 8	23	12	16
Writing (Editing & mechanics)	Grade 8	38	24	29
Writing (On-Demand)	Grade 8	28	15	24

Performing at or above JCPS or State Average

THE NECESSITY OF BLACK STUDENT ACTIVISM AND UNIONS IN PUBLIC SCHOOLS

BY GREG VANN
Specialist of Diversity, Equity, and Poverty, Jefferson County Public Schools

AMAYA WILLIAMS
Black Student Union (BSU) President, Fern Creek High School

History reflects the relentless efforts of Black student activism in shaping educational equality. From civil rights movements to current local initiatives, the advocacy for fair treatment, representation, and inclusiveness remain urgent. Despite great strides forward, challenges persist within Jefferson County Public Schools (JCPS).

Black students grapple with systemic barriers, facing disparities in almost every facet of life including disciplinary actions, unequal access to resources, and a curriculum often lacking their history and contributions. It's within this that Black Student Unions (BSUs) become a sense of hope, offering temples for communal support, Black cultural celebration, and academic excellence.

These unions, while providing a safe haven, also serve as platforms for advocacy. They encourage vital conversations about racial injustice, challenge the status quo, and cultivate leadership skills crucial for shaping a more equitable future for JCPS and Louisville at large. Their existence not only supports the immediate needs of Black students but also contributes to a better educational experience for all. However, the voices and experiences of Black students often go unheard, underscoring the pressing need for both activism and dedicated spaces like BSUs within public schools.

In the sections that follow, we amplify the voices and experiences of one BSU president who represents a body of students who deserve to be uplifted as the decision makers and change makers who will carry Louisville forward for decades to come. These are our future educators, politicians, and CEOs, and it's time for us to act like we know it.

AMAYA WILLIAMS, FERN CREEK HIGH SCHOOL BSU PRESIDENT:

As a bi-racial Fern Creek High School senior, I've challenged myself a lot during high school by taking rigorous courses. Throughout high school, I began to see that there weren't many people who looked like me in my advanced or AP classes. I was able to keep up with the work and passed my classes, but I felt out of place. A lot of my friends were either in totally different classes or in the honors classes and I wasn't able to see them much in my core classes. As I progressed through high school, I felt like I was distancing myself from my community as, at the time, I was only focusing on my academics and felt I didn't belong. I wanted to somehow be involved with something outside of academics. This want for involvement would allow me to discover the biggest impact in my high school career: our Black Student Union.

I attended my first meeting the week after I saw BSU posters around the school. Instantly, I felt like I belonged due to the sheer amount of diversity. Black Student Union allows us to share our stories and listen to one another as we can all relate in some way or another. We educate each other and help by attending or holding events that help to spread awareness. For instance, last February we were a part of Fern Creek's first-ever Black History Month Art Showcase, which displayed student and staff art and music and is now an annual event. We also created our very own spirit week, which helps to celebrate and represent our culture. We come together to support and look out for each other in a meaningful way. We also help out in our community. For example, for our culmination project last May, we donated a variety of art supplies to the Cabbage Patch Settlement House. Most importantly, BSU celebrates our excellence and success. As we continue through semesters, we congratulate our members and are happy for the efforts, achievements, and commitments they've made.

Black Student Union is teaching us not only to be proud of our culture, but to be a voice for it and help our community thrive. As a previous vice president and now president, I want these ideals and commitment toward educating, spreading awareness, and celebrating excellence to continue after I graduate. Despite the efforts toward prohibiting public school engagement in diversity, equity, inclusion, and belonging, it's important to note that BSU is serving as a safe space for students like me who feel like they don't belong in their school community — to gain a sense of belonging that is important for our youth today and in the future.

AS IT RELATES — BLACK LOUISVILLE AND RACIAL EQUITY: THE LESS AND MORE OF THE RACIAL EQUITY POLICY

JOHN DAVID MARSHALL, ED.D.
Chief Equity Officer
Jefferson County Public Schools

The state of Black Louisville, particularly the state of Black education, is and will always be under attack. The growing bombardment on Black thought is confusing, frightening, and abhorrent to some — mainly because positive Black thought begets progress. Progress begets truth. Truth begets balance.

In Jefferson County Public Schools (JCPS), the Racial Equity Policy has been a lever to beget betterment for all students over the last seven years. New and needed cogs to the system are in place, and they have yielded some positive change. It is safe to say that much more needs to be done. Further, what needs to be done cannot and should not rest with one department, one school system, or one superintendent. Met with some internal and external resistance, the policy has brought to light the truth of public education. It was never meant for Black people. Some legislators are working hard to maintain that which was meant. By banning books and diversity, equity, and inclusion (DEI) efforts, curtailing curriculum, and dismissing opportunities to make change, a wave of saboteurs, racists, Black cowards (in and outside of the field of education), and play-nice politicians work to stake claims of nightmarish nonsense — nonsense like public schools teach critical race theory, kids are being taught to hate each other, and the gap could close if schools just focused on literacy and numeracy.

At the core of the educational problem in America is the lie that school was designed for Black minds. Thus, when a policy that punches propaganda in the proverbial face attempts to sink and become fibrous, the war cry should bellow as loud as the roaring sea, "Strengthen racial equity in the school!" Black Louisville can strengthen its racial equity by:

- **Knowing what the policy is and what it should look like in action**
- **Knowing that every person in the schoolhouse is accountable for it**
- **Asking the critical question(s) about Black minds and Black bodies**
- **Demanding that it (racial equity) can be shown, touched, multiplied, and proven to be effective**

Diversity, equity, and inclusion as a theory is far from under attack. Diversity, equity, and inclusion with stipulations is as American as the schoolhouse that had no intention on teaching Black bodies — while breaking Black bodies. More than 75 percent of inclusion officers are white, meaning whiteness is never at war with itself. The momentum of truth and the pen of progress that seek to move theory to action is the pain of the happy-to-be-asleep, anti-woke coward and racist. Diversity, equity and inclusion as a nice, fluffy pillow is not a threat.

Tools and documents designed to improve racial equity — such as the Racial Equity Policy, the Affirming Racial Equity Tool, the Equity Screener, The Racial Equity Analysis Protocol, the Equity Monitoring Progress Tool, the Equity Scorecard,[1] and the Leading with Equity, Accountability, Support, and Expectations[2] — stir the distilled meaning of diversity and inclusion. If and when these are used faithfully, coupled with deep personal introspection, gaps will close.

At the 2023 Louisville Urban League Impact Luncheon, President and CEO Lyndon Pryor stated, "Louisville is so far, yet so close to getting it right." That is hauntingly true. For Black Louisville, as far as education goes, public schools are still our best option. Public policy that is enforced is still one of our biggest levers. Jefferson County Public Schools need to be expected to teach better than ever before. Other entities need to do the rest. Performative press conferences and head nodding do nothing. Politicians need to go. Racists and racism need to be identified, vilified, and left aside.

The state of Black Louisville, education included, is in need of more and less. More support and demand for racial equity. More "woke" educators. More funding for Black minds. More impatience. We need less lip service, fewer meetings, less white pandering, less comfortability, and less talk.

Less and more! There is your numeracy lesson for the day. Add DEI(real work) while subtracting lazy, lethal legislation and petrified pretenders (Black and white) who maintain the mangling of Black minds and bodies.

THE STATE OF THE DISTRICT 2024

DR. CORRIE SHULL, CHAIR
Jefferson County Public Schools (JCPS) Board of Education

Among the most memorable insights made by James Baldwin — the extraordinary novelist, thinker, and social critic — is his assertion that "to be Negro in this country and to be relatively conscious is to be in a rage almost all of the time."[1] Baldwin's insight perfectly applies to even the most passive observers of the politics surrounding public education — both nationally and locally — especially those who cherish public education as the cornerstone of a flourishing democratic society.

The current battle for public education is enough to work anyone into fits of rage. Nationally, assaults on public education include banning books, dictating what teachers can teach, and passing legislative measures to allow and encourage teachers to be armed in classrooms. In Kentucky, these assaults take a more subtle form, expressed through the Kentucky General Assembly's refusal to fully fund public education, the continued attempt to use taxpayer dollars to fund private schools, and the exceptionally damaging initiative to explore breaking up the Jefferson County Public School (JCPS) district, which would undoubtedly create a district of haves and have-nots.

Exacerbating an already intense state of affairs for public education, on April 10th, 2024, the Jefferson County Board of Education voted to remove transportation for magnet, traditional, and non-resides Academies of Louisville students. This decision was made without regard for the most recent Transportation Audit Report conducted by the Prismatic Company of North Carolina, which argued that removing transportation for these students was not necessary to overcome the district's transportation challenges.[2] Perhaps the most insulting aspect of this ordeal was the intentional exclusion of community voice and collaboration.

District officials have argued that they have had difficulty finding drivers; however, as of this writing, the district has only hosted three hiring blitzes targeting bus drivers, despite this shortage being foreseeable for quite some time. Removing transportation for any group of students does not increase access or make the district more equitable. It is an affront to the decades of work by current and past district professionals and community partners to ensure equity and access within JCPS.

While the district touts higher graduation rates bolstered by an increased representation of students who are college and/or career ready, there must be vigilance among community members and district officials to ensure that the district does not re-segregate or prevent students and families from accessing desired opportunities. Community members and organizations passionate about public education and equity must insist on collaboration with the district on every issue, as all issues within public education impact our children. The best minds must consistently come together to develop creative and sustainable plans to overcome the myriad of challenges facing the district, and pave a pathway to a more excellent future for public education.

We, as a community, must refuse to return to historic patterns of segregation and decreased opportunities for the most vulnerable in Louisville. The JCPS district and Louisville community are at a precipice that requires inclusivity, honesty, competence, and collaboration. Insisting that JCPS be its best is not merely advocacy for a school system, but a commitment to the principles of equity, opportunity, and the very future of Louisville.

For those who love public education and its promise of providing diverse opportunities for students, the current state of affairs is certainly concerning. However, we must not give up or give in to apathy; we must lift our voices and advocate until the school system that is charged with serving all students does just that in the most excellent way.

"...ON APRIL 10TH, 2024, THE JEFFERSON COUNTY BOARD OF EDUCATION VOTED TO REMOVE TRANSPORTATION FOR MAGNET, TRADITIONAL, AND NON-RESIDES ACADEMIES OF LOUISVILLE STUDENTS...PERHAPS THE MOST INSULTING ASPECT OF THIS ORDEAL WAS THE INTENTIONAL EXCLUSION OF COMMUNITY VOICE AND COLLABORATION."

ANTI-RACIST AND WHITE: WHAT DEP OFFERS TO ADDRESS WHITE SUPREMACY

RACHEL KLEIN
Specialist of Anti-Racist Pedagogy
Jefferson County Public Schools

Anti-racism in Jefferson County Public Schools (JCPS) is an action-based response to racist policies, practices, systems, and beliefs that exist within education. It focuses intently on instruction, curriculum, and pedagogy as liberatory means to decenter whiteness. It exposes and includes the histories, texts, contributions, perspectives, and experiences of mis- and underrepresented people, filling in gaps that previously existed in our collective knowledge. Anti-racism is disruptive in nature, requiring input and effort across stakeholder groups. In adherence to the Racial Equity Policy, "The Board commits the District to promoting the success of all students and work actively to eliminate institutional and structural policies and practices that perpetuate inequities among racial groups and thereby contribute to disproportionality of access and outcomes."[1]

I am a white woman pursuing and supporting anti-racist policies and practices across JCPS. My positionality and how it relates to my professional perspectives may not be what first comes to mind when considering who fills the role of an Anti-Racist specialist in JCPS. However, racism and white supremacy negatively impact everyone, white people included. Laying these monumental entities at the feet of Black and Brown people and asking them to find solutions to their own oppression is obviously not the answer, so here I stand, squarely committed to help form the future state of anti-racism in JCPS. I am reminded of my whiteness every day, and I keep this reminder close each day as I work with my colleagues to upend systemic inequities in educational outcomes and opportunities for our most marginalized students in JCPS. I am faced with not just my own whiteness, but also the pervasive whiteness that seeps into so much of culture, society, expectations, policies, and systems. The role I play in all of this is quite complex, and at times concerns of participating in white saviorism, or the act of swooping in from my privileged position to help Black and Brown people who never declared that they needed saving, plague me. I do not wish for my actions and allyship to be accused of this, but I am human, therefore not without flaw or bias. I have likely failed at times in my approach to anti-racism, but I learn from my missteps and push forward anyway.

I understand that many white educators and leaders are fearful of claiming they are an anti-racist ally, just to falter or make mistakes along the way. I have felt that, I will feel that, and I will remain vulnerable in my work if it means being a model for those who look like me but do not know where to start. And while no amount of reading or researching about the history, experiences, contributions, and cultures of Black and Brown people will ever provide me lived experience, it is imperative for me to pursue this knowledge if I am to be a true anti-racist ally. This knowledge is abundant and accessible, and I stand with my colleagues in the Department of Diversity, Equity, and Poverty (DEP) to support collective growth, awareness, reflection, and learning as they relate to not just envisioning but enacting an anti-racist stance in education across all of JCPS.

There is still much work to be done to bring the Racial Equity Policy to full fruition, which requires accountability across all JCPS departments and roles. I am pleased to share many of the learning opportunities, resources, and tools provided by DEP that address white supremacy and anti-racism in our district. These include:

NAACP community forums:
Routine opportunities co-hosted by the local chapter of the National Association for the Advancement of Colored People (NAACP) and DEP to provide the community updates and information about the impact of racial equity in JCPS.

Speaker series:
Routine opportunities that feature presentations from local and national experts in education. Speakers lead professional-development sessions for JCPS teachers and administrators that focus on many issues facing our students and ways to better reach them.

Implicit bias modules:
A four-part deep dive for JCPS teachers and administrators to explore and address their implicit biases.

Reckoning with Racism series:
Guidance documents for educators regarding current events, derogatory language, Black culture and art, and more.

Equity Monitoring Progress Tool (EMPT):
A school-generated, district-evaluated report used to gauge how and to what degree individual schools are meeting the expectations of the JCPS Racial Equity Policy. It is used year-round to provide more robust systems of support as they are needed to individual schools. EMPTs provide a snapshot of work done across a single academic year.

Implicit bias modules Affiriming Racial Equity (ARE) Tool:
A planning document to be utilized throughout the Professional Learning Community (PLC) planning process to ensure all classroom educators are consciously and purposefully incorporating racially equitable content and practices into their daily pedagogy and practices.

Racial Equity Analysis Protocol (REAP):
An instrument to be used when school leadership is making decisions that impact students. The expectation is that this protocol is used for every said decision. In turn, should the screening of an idea or initiative (un)intentionally marginalize or negatively impact a group of students, leadership is to adjust the idea/plan, "run" the idea through the REAP again, and check inclusion.

Equity Scorecard:

The Equity Scorecard provides real-time data on academic proficiency, suspension, attendance, transition readiness, access and opportunity, and teacher demographics for the district. The data are disaggregated by race and gender, so users can observe the performance by group.

Equity Screener:

A tool utilized as part of the school leadership selection process that calls for JCPS staff to address the historical marginalization and disproportionate outcomes of students of color. The Equity Screener establishes an expectation that all JCPS staff should be willing, able, and proven to lead with equity in mind. Candidates seeking school leadership positions (principal, assistant principal, counselors) will be required to provide evidence of their competencies and demonstrated actions across four dispositions.

Louisville Teacher Residency:

A community-wide certification pathway that aims to increase the pipeline of minority candidates certified to teach in JCPS and increase teacher retention for our Accelerated Improvement Schools (AIS).

Curricular and instructional resources:

A variety of resources that are closely aligned with the expectations of the JCPS Racial Equity Policy and breathe life into the curricular and instructional components of the ARE Tool.

Racism hotline:

A hotline to report instances of discrimination, racism, and/or harmful behavior.

Envision Equity magazine:

A monthly digital publication featuring articles, spotlights, resources, and more that align with the Racial Equity Policy.

Battery of Opportunities:

A yearly listing of DEP-sponsored learning opportunities, professional development sessions, book studies, and events that JCPS teachers and administrators can engage with that enhance their knowledge and awareness of the needs of their students and families.

As a supporter of using one's voice to advocate for themselves and others, I encourage readers to consider what it means to advocate for the work of racial equity in our schools so that it can, in turn, thrive in our community. Knowing what tools exist for schools and staff to turn to when faced with critical decisions that impact student achievement is an important step towards advocating for their use. Another is to be in community with the schools in our community. There are so many roles to play as it relates to supporting equitable learning environments across our schools, and our students deserve your voice and advocacy. Whether this is in the form of parental representation on school-based decision making committees, attending and speaking at Board of Education mMeetings, or offering your gifts as a guest speaker, there is a place for you to support the vision of a racially equitable JCPS.

DEDICATION TO DIANE PORTER

JOHN DAVID MARSHALL ED.D
Chief Equity Officer
Jefferson. County Public Schools

There are those leaders who come around once in a decade (or even longer) who are so maternally strong, so maternally in tune, and so unbelievably passionate for community and children that the feats and fights the person endured are almost that of lore and legend. What Dr. Diane Porter has done and tried to do to improve the state of Black Louisville, particularly for Black students, should not go unnoticed.

It never failed. One of two statements would harmoniously be shared in almost any and every meeting that she attended. They were, " For the students that look like me..." and/or "In the district that I represent..." Simple to say; however, hard to mean it. Dr. Porter said it and meant it. Dr. Porter loves Jefferson County Public Schools, the West End of Louisville, and all the children that live in this city. But let us be clear, Black children tug(ged) on her big heartstrings in a way that only a mother could understand.

As she sat, beautifully and bravely in her Board of Education seat, she toted a picture of her daughter Danielle Porter, as well as pictures,letters and emails from parents, students, and staff. Those items explained who she is: a mother to many.

This section of the State of Black Louisville is respectfully dedicated to Dr. Diane Porter. May her vision and love and light forever be a model of might and reflection of righteousness.

ABC

“

IT NEEDS TO BE MADE CLEAR THAT BLACK FOLKS ARE NOT TO BLAME FOR THE ENVIRONMENTAL INJUSTICES TO WHICH WE HAVE BEEN AND ARE BEING SUBJECTED. WE ARE, HOWEVER, THE PEOPLE WHO MUST BE PART OF THE SOLUTION.

EBONI COCHRAN

HOW BLACK FARMING COOPERATIVE COULD HELP SOLVE LOUISVILLE'S FOOD CRISIS

LOUISVILLE URBAN LEAGUE'S TEAM KILIMO

Louisville's food crisis is not different from that of any other city across this nation. There has been collective work in identifying the issues and presenting solutions, but implementation has been slow due to various reasons such as funding and strategic collaboration for sustainability.

The COVID-19 pandemic exposed vulnerabilities in our food system, especially for marginalized communities like Black Americans and single-living seniors. To address this, we must teach Black people to produce their own food and revive historical cooperative models for economic empowerment. Agricultural cooperatives, rooted in collective ownership and democratic decision-making, have historically empowered Black farmers and communities. Learning from those past practices can equip Black people with tools for sustainable food production and economic independence.

The statistics are staggering. According to the U.S. Bureau of Labor Statistics (BLS), in April 2020, the U.S. unemployment rate hit 14.8%, leaving millions without jobs.[1] This worsened economic disruption and food insecurity as many grocery stores closed — both independently owned as well as corporate structures. This underscores the urgent need for sustainable solutions, empowering communities to control their food sources and economic futures.

From a wider lens, we can see that Louisville's food system is broken from production all the way to waste prevention. Our city officials must examine the root problems associated with food and build an ecosystem that, over time, mitigates the violence, health, and economic issues we are all facing. Our prior experiences have revealed that at-risk Black Americans – notably youth and single-living seniors — face significant barriers in accessing nutritious food. Despite government efforts to provide spaces for food production like community gardens, this provision usually comes with a lack of follow-up resources and support that hinders communities from sustaining and expanding these given spaces. This continues cycles of poverty and dependency, necessitating comprehensive strategies to address immediate and long-term challenges.

The Louisville Urban League's Team Kilimo aims to be more of a resource to urban farmers and gardeners by operating as a fellowship with collective strategies. The inaugural team is made up of long standing community collaborators and urban farm business leaders. We teach Black people of Louisville Metro the basics to starting and sustaining their projects while connecting them to additional support across the city.

Historically, agricultural cooperatives have offered a promising pathway to address challenges like those faced in Louisville. The Louisville Urban League may not be starting these cooperatives, but it supports the base knowledge and initial resource through a fellowship program built around the principles of Sankofa, an African proverb that encourages us to build our future with what we've learned from our past. We use these principles to equip Black youth and seniors with knowledge and skills for sustainable farming practices. Project Kilimo emphasizes education and hands-on experiences, resulting in individual and community food production and soil regeneration on previously unusable land.

Our call to action is simple:

- **Advocate for increased support and resources for Black-led agricultural initiatives like Project Kilimo, focusing on youth and seniors.**
- **Invest in advancing educational programs teaching sustainable farming and reviving cooperative models for economic empowerment.**
- **Volunteer with Project Kilimo in creating access to nutritious food and building community-owned food production projects.**
- **Support policies prioritizing equity and addressing systemic barriers to healthy food access.**
- **Raise awareness about the importance of collective action in constructing resilient and equitable food systems.**

If we spark curiosity by reintroducing our cultural history of cooperative farming practices, we can build a better, sustainable future for our communities.

PARENTING WHILE BLACK

ARMON R. PERRY, PH.D., MSW
University of Louisville, Kent School of Social Work and Family Science

CHERI LANGLEY, PH.D., MPH, CHES
Walden University, College of Health Professions

Family is the primary institution in society. In addition to the provision of material needs, the family also shapes its members through nurturance and socialization. For parents, bearing these responsibilities can be stress provoking. Having to do so while combatting racism and discrimination only magnifies the stress.[1] Given the research indicating that parental stress is associated with negative outcomes,[2] investigating the sources and impacts of stress is important to our understanding of family functioning — particularly for Black families who are more likely to be negatively impacted by racism. To examine these issues, we conducted a mixed methods study featuring a quantitative survey and qualitative interviews.

STUDY METHODS

The survey collected data from Black parents in Louisville who were raising at least one minor child. The survey inquired into a range of topics related to parenting including the parents' report of the quality of their relationship with their child, the disciplinary techniques employed by parents, and their parenting efficacy (i.e. the parent's belief in their ability to perform the roles associated with parenting successfully). The survey also collected data on an array of factors shaping the respondents' parenting such as mental health, co-parenting support, social support and their experiences with racism. A total of 129 participants responded: 67% reported being mothers, 32% reported being fathers, and 1% reported being grandparents. On average, the participants had 2.26 children and there was a wide range of socioeconomic statuses represented. With regard to household income, 22.5%reported an annual household income of less than $35,000; 56.6% reported an annual household income between $35,000-$99,999, and 20.9%reported an annual household income of over $100,000. There were also 36 zip codes represented. In addition to the quantitative analyses, a subset of study participants participated in individual, qualitative interviews. A total of 27 interviews were conducted that lasted an hour, on average. The interviews served to take an in-depth look into the participants' lived experiences as parents to learn more about the circumstances impacting their thinking and behavior as Black parents.

RESULTS

Data analyses revealed a statistically significant and inverse relationship between parents' report of their experiences with racism and their parent-child relationship quality, parenting efficacy, and use of disciplinary techniques. In other words, parents who reported being involved in more frequent racist or discriminatory encounters also reported lower scores for the quality of their relationship with their children; they reported lower levels of confidence in their ability to parent successfully; and they reported using harsher techniques to discipline their children.

An examination of the qualitative interview data corroborated these findings and offered some additional insight into how they manifested in parents' lives. Each interview started with questions related to the respondents' parenting goals and philosophies. In doing so, we sought to delve into the parents' perspectives on what they were attempting to accomplish through their parenting. An emergent theme from the interview data was that many of the parents mentioned they were choosing to prioritize their children's happiness and mental health. Often, this was in direct response to what they perceived as their own parents' prioritizing economic upward mobility. In these cases, parents were concerned about the mental and emotional price their kids would have to pay if they emphasized getting a good job and making money over everything else the For example, a father of two stated:

"Man, I just want my kids to be healthy, productive human beings in society. I want them to be healthy and happy. I want them to be able to give something back to the world, as kind of, their payment to the world, if you will. Use what they've got to give back to the world. I'm always encouraging my kids to look inside, their gifts, their passions, what are their interests and then, 'How can I cultivate that and make that something healthy and beautiful, even if it's something that I don't completely understand?' But that's where I'm at. I want them to be healthy. I want them to be happy."

However, despite their interests in wanting to make sure their children were safe and happy, many of the parents found themselves preoccupied with the fallout from racism. For some, dealing with racism literally meant confronting people and situations that they felt were discriminatory or grounded in prejudice and stereotypes. For example, one mother lamented having to advocate for her son because, as one of very few Black students attending his private school, he was automatically assumed to be the aggressor in a situation where he was defending himself against an attack perpetrated by other students. In other cases, parents agonized over trying to pinpoint the right time to begin preparing their children for the impact of racism to protect them from what they felt was inevitable, while also not wanting to project their previous pain and traumas onto their children unnecessarily. An illustration of this was a single mother responding to being asked if she had specific strategies to help her children navigate being Black in America. In sharing her experience, she offered:

"Specific strategies? That's a hard one. Everything is tied to being Black in America to me. Now, I'm not going to say that I walk around and say, 'This is your white friend. You're Black and you need to be careful.' But I definitely make sure that they know who they are, and that they always remember that."

Like many of the respondents we interviewed, the parent is trying to strike the difficult balance between doing her due diligence regarding racial socialization and not being a racial alarmist. This struggle was consistent with the narratives of many other parents who reported struggling with things like knowing that as their children got older, the broader society would treat them like adults and not give them grace; wanting their children to have a cultural identity and sense of belonging, but knowing that Black people are not monolithic in thought or ideology; whether or how to teach their children to code switch; and helping their children understand the impacts of being Black while also appreciating their intersectional identities.

In sum, perhaps the most salient finding from the study was that, almost by definition, parenting while Black meant that parents did not have the privilege to simply develop and implement their parenting philosophies to promote our children's healthy growth and development. Rather, for Black parents, due to the insidiousness of racism, raising their children had the potential to be an emotionally draining task that led to feelings of anger, frustration, or disillusionment. This occurred as parents were compelled to dedicate portions of their finite mental, emotional, and financial resources to preparing for and responding to the challenges brought on by racism. In this way, they found themselves spending less time parenting in response to their children's needs and more time parenting in response to the real or perceived constraints and restrictions superimposed on them by the broader society.

CALL TO ACTION

The findings from this study amplify the reality that racism still represents a significant challenge to Black families. To be specific, it highlights the difficulties that Black parents face in trying to navigate everyday life while providing for and nurturing their children. In recent years, a light has been shone on Louisville. In this process, Louisville has been re-cast from its reputation as a progressive oasis in a sea of conservatism to perhaps a more accurate description of a simply less overtly racist city within the larger pantheon of other hostile places and spaces. This means that despite the Louisville Urban League's noteworthy contributions to the progress and empowerment of Black Louisville, there remains yet more work. In fact, the work now is as complicated as it's ever been because the within-group diversity that exists across contemporary Black Louisville means that coming to consensus on an agenda for change that encompasses all of the relevant constituencies is as difficult as it's ever been. History has proven that there will be no Superman coming to save us and contemporary times reveal that the past is not as far behind us as we'd like to believe. Therefore, it is recommended that the League integrate sense of community into the work across its existing pillars of jobs, justice, education, housing, and business to ensure that the spirit of mutual aid and Black self-reliance remain driving forces catalyzing our movements toward full and sustainable inclusion.

ACKNOWLEDGEMENT:

Funding for this project was provided by Walden University, grant number FRIG-2021-14.

THE STATE OF ENVIRONMENTAL JUSTICE

EBONI COCHRAN

The state of Black Louisville as it relates to environmental justice is dire. Our air, water, and soil have been contaminated. These are the very things we rely on for our very existence.

For decades, residents in numerous neighborhoods have been adversely impacted by toxic chemicals emitted from a cluster of chemical facilities commonly referred to as "Rubbertown." There have been excess emissions, explosions, fires, nauseous odors, and acute and chronic illness and deaths — some of which residents and academics have attributed to Rubbertown.[1] Railcars also pose a major risk as it relates to derailments and the leaking of hazardous chemicals. The train derailment that caused a toxic fire in East Palestine, Ohio could easily happen here.[2]

Additional pathways of exposure to harmful chemicals include but are not limited to:

- **Legacy pollution from the Duke Energy Gallagher Station power plant**
- **Dioxin in Chickasaw Park**
- **Whiskey fungus, odors, and noise from Heaven Hill's Bernheim Distillery**
- **Particulate matter/ wood dust and thick black smoke coming from Anderson Wood Products**
- **Toxic pollution from Clariant - West**
- **Soil contamination from the former Black Leaf Chemical site**

This is not to mention incidents associated with the Louisville Metropolitan Sewer District (MSD), like the spill that occurred on August 5th, 2023 involving a leaking tank, which resulted in an order for residents to shelter in place.[3]

Much of the local discussion revolves around odors. Over the last several years, there has been a push to attribute all odors to the sewer system. The Air Pollution Control District (APCD) and MSD have yet to provide a good explanation about how odors from the sewer system are differentiated from odors coming from chemical facilities. Even more serious are some of the chemicals associated with the odors. What about chemicals we may not be able to detect, but are harmful nonetheless?

Chemicals emitted from Rubbertown are associated with health problems that affect every biological system.[4] Rubbertown facilities release chemicals with serious impacts:

- **Respiratory issues**
- **Cardiovascular issues**
- **Adverse effects to the reproductive system**
- **Nervous system issues**
- **Cancers**
- **Endocrine disruptors**
- **Developmental issues**

Rubbertown also emits teratogens and mutagens. A teratogen is a substance that causes birth defects by damaging the fetus. A mutagen is a substance that causes mutations. It causes a change in the genetic material within a body's cell. This can lead to birth defects, miscarriages, or cancer.[5]

As with all of these impacts, the impact of climate change on communities at the fence line of industry is a subject that needs to be explored more intensely and with immediacy. Unfortunately, there is no sense of urgency because we, Black people, are seen as expendable. According to Dr. Robert Bullard, Distinguished Professor of Urban Planning and Environmental Policy at Texas Southern University, "Race is still more potent than income in predicting the distribution of pollution and polluting facilities."[6]

Black smoke from Anderson Wood, located in the Parkland Neighborhood. Photo taken provided by Rubbertown Emergency ACTion (REACT)
Photo Credit: @reactlouisville

This city is failing Black Louisville. Some of these failings include:

- **Catering to the chemical industry**
- **Lack of effective odor investigations**
- **Lack of fight to protect local control of air toxics**
- **Inadequate planning as its relates to climate change**
- **Lack of community training in emergency preparedness**
- **Lack of effective air monitoring**
- **Lack of courage among decision makers**
- **Excluding impacted communities from helping to create effective plans and solutions**

Black people are tired. We are tired from generations of fighting for basic rights and our mere existence. We need to pull from the strength of our ancestors, those folks who were tired beyond what we can imagine but still fought for us. They did what they needed to do to push us this far. Now it is our turn.

It may sound cliche to repeat that Black people must come together, but it is true and necessary. This pulling together requires a level of self-analysis that many of us seldom engage in. Are we willing to lose the individualistic mindset in exchange for thinking of solutions for the whole? Are we willing to see our people through a healthy lens and not through the eyes of the oppressor? One of my favorite passages from James Baldwin is:

"They saw themselves as others had seen them. They had been formed by images made of them by those who had had the deepest necessity to despise them."[7]

WE must see ourselves through a healthy enough lens to work together for the good of the whole. We must fight against this wickedness without ceasing. Is it our fight, alone? Absolutely not. As we hold others accountable, we must also coordinate like we never have before. We have the intelligence, we have the right, and we have our ancestors rooting for us.

It needs to be made clear that Black folks are not to blame for the environmental injustices to which we have been and are being subjected. We are, however, the people who must be part of the solution.

No one is coming to save us. We must save ourselves.

HOUSING

"

TODAY, HOUSEHOLDS WITH A BLACK RESIDENT MAKE UP **13.6% OF ALL HOUSEHOLDS** BUT HOLD **ONLY 4.7% OF ALL WEALTH.** AND THE MEDIAN WEALTH OF HOUSEHOLDS WITH BLACK RESIDENTS IS **$24,520,** COMPARED TO **$250,400** FOR HOUSEHOLDS WITH WHITE RESIDENTS.

JOHN D. BORDERS, JR.

1954 TO 2024: ON THE 70TH ANNIVERSARY OF THE WADE-BRADEN CASE

ANGELA STOREY, PH.D.
Director, Anne Braden Institute for Social Justice Research, Associate Professor, Department of Anthropology, University of Louisville

This year marks the 70th anniversary of the Wade-Braden case, a series of events that highlighted the state of racialized housing inequality, white supremacist violence, and attempts to discredit the civil rights movement through McCarthy-era red scare tactics of 1950s Louisville. Housing inequality and racist violence persist in Louisville, but one legacy of the Wade-Braden case is that the city also remains a center for vibrant and hopeful local activism for fair and affordable housing.

In the spring of 1954, Andrew Wade — a Black, World War II, U.S. Navy veteran — approached Anne and Carl Braden to seek their assistance in purchasing a home. Andrew and his wife Charlotte were expecting their second child and had been seeking a home in one of Louisville's burgeoning suburbs for their young family. Despite having the means to purchase the home they sought, the Wades had been blocked time and time again by the racist practices of realtors, an experience faced by many other Black, would-be, suburban homeowners. But, Andrew Wade persisted. He strategically approached the Bradens, a white couple involved in local civil rights and labor campaigns, to make the purchase of a home in Shively on his behalf and then to transfer the title to him.

In May of that year, the Bradens did just that and the Wades moved into their new home. What followed were compounding forms of violent action and rhetoric, as white residents reacted to the presence of a Black family in their neighborhood. Shot at, called names, attacked in the press and, ultimately, targeted by a charge of dynamite set off under the bedroom window of their young daughter (neither she nor anyone else was injured), the Wades reluctantly left their damaged, unlivable home. That summer, the Bradens and five other white activists who had supported the Wades were charged with sedition and put on trial, allegedly part of a communist conspiracy to create social tension that would overthrow the state government. Once her husband was released from the prison sentence he received for the purchase, Anne Braden detailed the unfolding events of the wider case in her 1958 book "The Wall Between." The case profoundly influenced her realization, as a white woman, of the grip of white supremacy held on this community — seen in both the violences and exclusions that the Wades faced, and also the extreme actions taken by the state government to repress activism.

The story of the case and its relevance to housing activism in Louisville is much longer and its impacts ripple outward far more broadly than what I can capture in this short essay. The legacy of the Bradens has been one of persistent activism to end housing discrimination and white supremacy, but the events for which they are best known were not ones in which they acted alone to seek social change. Indeed, the incredible courage of the Wade family to make a home for themselves, the bravery of many activists to stay in the home with them, and the national support from multi-racial C=civil rights and civil liberties organizations during the resulting trial show what social change requires: a wide cast of actors willing to persist in the face of sustained repression.

One of the legacies of the Wade-Braden case is in its name. Although naming only the Wades and Bradens does not capture the breadth of a movement, remembering the joint actions of these two families does remind us that social change is never achieved in isolation. Change requires the daring of those who, together, see other possible futures. Andrew Wade saw and acted to make real the possibility of a life for families like his in a suburban home. Anne and Carl Braden saw and acted to make real the possibility of racial solidarity. Although we can also see the legacy of this case in the persistence of housing segregation today, the racist violence that upholds unjust systems, and the difficulty of making change, I also see the light that the Wades, Bradens, and their friends shone ahead onto a path towards justice that many continue to light for us— in Louisville and beyond.

Based on her own activism, Mariama Kaba writes, "Hope is a discipline." It seems to me that the Wades and Bradens would have agreed, and that their actions to make change are a call to keep enacting the hope of a future that we do not yet fully see. They acted not in the naïve way of those who have yet to grasp the massive structural foundations that uphold our racist systems. Instead, they acted in the courageous way of people who see those structures, work to dismantle them, and then seek to build, anew, a more just world.

Louisville is home to many activists who continue to build the path towards housing justice, including many whose names fill the pages of this report. There is no limit to the cast of actors needed to make change, though, and being securely housed does not remove you from the fight for fair housing. Find your own way into this struggle by connecting with groups doing this work locally, from the Louisville Urban League and the Metropolitan Housing Coalition to movements doing tenant's rights work, seeking equitable changes to zoning laws, and supporting anti-displacement in neighborhoods at threat from gentrification.

Related Readings

- ***Kaba, Mariame. 2021. We Do This 'Til We Free Us: Abolitionist Organizing and Transforming Justice. Chicago: Haymarket Books.***

- ***Fosl, Catherine. 2002. Subversive Southerner: Anne Braden and the Struggle for Racial Justice in the Cold War South. Lexington: University of Kentucky Press.***

- ***Braden, Anne. 1999 (1958). The Wall Between. Knoxville: University of Tennessee Press.***

LOUISVILLE NEEDS MORE HOUSING DIVERSITY

TONY CURTIS
Executive Director, Metropolitan Housing Coalition

CASSIA HERRON
Urban Planning Consultant

Like many U.S. cities, Louisville faces significant challenges in housing its residents. The city lacks housing diversity across all Metro Council districts, affecting the ability of thousands of individuals and families to access safe, fair, and affordable housing.

Under Mayor Greg Fischer, the Louisville Metro Government's 2019 Housing Needs Assessment documented the need for 31,412 housing units affordable to households making 30% Area Median Income (AMI) The updated 2024 Housing Needs Assessment shows an increase in the unmet need to 36,160 housing units. Soon into Mayor Craig Greenberg's term, he announced plans to build 15,000 units of housing in his *My Louisville Home.*[1] The plan also promises that Metro Government will:

1. Revise the Land Development Code (LDC) to increase density and streamline the development approval process

2. Increase funding for the Louisville Affordable Housing Trust Fund (LAHTF)

3. Implement new financing streams that enable the Louisville Metro Housing Authority to invest in the production of new units and prioritize energy efficiency

4. Create long-term affordable homeownership opportunities with non-profit development partners; and

5. Incentivize the reuse of vacant and abandoned properties

With a collective community understanding of the need, Louisville Metro's offices of Planning, Codes & Regulations, and Housing and Community Development, as well as Metro Council, have consistently attempted to address the city's housing needs with active input from citizens, housing advocates, and developers alike. The growing presence of a houseless population on the streets and within the Jefferson County Public School district exacerbates the need to enhance the city's existing housing stock and accelerate the production of a diversity of new housing across the city.

The Louisville Metro Council took two important actions in 2020 that created the conditions for change.

The first step LMC took was to pass a fair housing ordinance expanding protected classes against discriminatory housing practices to include arrest or conviction history, homeless status, source of income, or military service record.[2] The source of income protections came under attack during the 2024 Kentucky Legislative Session with the passage of House Bill 18, which overturned Louisville's source of income protections and prevented other municipalities from passing similar legislation.[3] This is a huge step backwards and deserves a legal challenge in the courts.

The second action LMC took was in response to Louisville's Plan 2040 — the city's comprehensive plan guiding growth and development over the next 20 years that contained fair and affordable housing for the first time.[4] The Louisville Metro Council passed a resolution ordering a review of Louisville's outdated and discriminatory Land Development Code (LDC) using an equity lens. The LDC tells us what you can build, where you can build it and, ultimately, where someone can live. The resulting 2021 LDC reform recommendations are categorized into three phases:[5]

- **Phase 1: Accessory Dwelling Units (ADUs), community and market gardens, and public notice requirements**
- **Phase 2: Middle Housing to increase diverse types of housing**
- **Phase 3: Inclusionary Zoning and Environmental Justice Review Criteria**

Phase 1 recommendations were early wins and adopted on June 24, 2021. Phase 2 focused on middle housing and is currently being considered. Metro Planning staff remains available to receive public feedback as the ordinance makes its way through the legislative process. Phase 3 recommendations are set to be vetted as a part of a new Metro Council Ad Hoc Land Use Committee in the near future. All of these actions will expand housing opportunity and choice across all 26 Metro Council districts.

LDC REFORM	HOW WOULD THIS INCREASE HOUSING DENSITY?	STATUS AS OF JULY 2024
Accessory Dwelling Units (ADUs)	ADUs allow for the building of an additional unit on a lot zoned for and contains a single-family house.	PASSED
Inclusionary Zoning	Middle housing allows for the building of duplexes, triplexes, fourplexes, townhouses, walking courts, and cottage courts. It allows for more units per lot in an area zoned for single-family housing (as long as certain criteria are met).	In process
Middle Housing	Inclusionary zoning would mandate that a certain percentage of affordable housing units be included in any development of a certain size as determined by Louisville Metro Council.	Being discussed at Metro Council Ad Hoc Land Use Committee
Environmental Justice Review Criteria	An environmental justice review increases the quality of housing, mitigates environmental harm and decreases housing displacement.	TBD

At the state level, a plethora of bills moved through the legislature that would have impacted the housing landscape. The following are the few good bills that ultimately did not pass:

HCR 68 would have established the Kentucky Housing Task Force to discuss and file a report on a variety of housing topics between the 2024 and 2025 legislative sessions.[6]

The Legislature did create a "Special Committee Kentucky Housing Task Force" of legislators to meet in the interim before the 2025 session.[7]

HB 102 would have had broad-ranging implications on statewide planning and zoning laws, effectively ending single-family zoning statewide, and would have supported Louisville's efforts in relation to land development code and zoning reforms.[8]

HB 76 would have updated the Uniform Residential Landlord Tenant Act (URLTA) and created urban-rural connections by defining the landlord and tenant relationship evenly across the Commonwealth.[9]

HB 466 would have prohibited property hoarding from-out-of-town developers acquired at master commissioners sales.[10]

There are also renewed efforts on eviction expungement, landlord duties with respect to abandoned property, and preventing electric and gas disconnections in extreme weather conditions. All of these proposed bills would have a positive impact on the ability of Louisvillians and citizens across the Commonwealth to secure and retain housing.

In the last few days of the General Assembly, the legislature passed HB 388 with an amendment that, in addition to making the mayoral and Metro Council races non-partisan, temporarily limits consolidated local governments from amending zoning classifications in their land development codes.[11] House Bill 88 also asks the mayor of the consolidated local government to review the make-up of the planning commission and processes for amendments related to residential zoning. This bill creates barriers to the ongoing work Louisville Metro Government and its stakeholders are currently undertaking to increase housing diversity across the city.

If Louisville is going to house its residents in proper order, it is essential that the citizenry is actively involved in informing our elected officials of what's needed. Public voices help elected officials understand the full scope and nuances of the housing crisis.

There are two ways for residents, advocates, and developers to participate:

1. **Engage Metro Council members and state legislators.**

Citizens are encouraged to be registered voters (if possible) and get to know their elected representatives. Call or send them an email to introduce yourself and to express concerns. Schedule a meeting in the district to get to know them. Show up at their events and support their interests. Engaging elected officials is an effective way to have your voice heard and seek understanding and/or compromise on issues.

2. Attend public meetings.
Metro Council has full council meetings every other Thursday and committee meetings on the weeks in between. While guests must be invited to speak at committee meetings, residents are able to sign up with the Council Clerk in advance to speak for up to 3 minutes at the full council meeting. Likewise, the Planning Commission and Board of Zoning and Adjustments offer opportunities for residents to speak about cases before the boards. Residents can also send emails and letters to Council members in relation to an ordinance or development project that needs Council or other approvals.

Though Metro Council and LMG officials are making progress, affordable housing advocates face a challenging policy landscape at all levels of government moving into 2024. Louisville has always had opponents of fair and affordable housing, but the opposition to fixing the problem continues to grow. Some opposition to multi-family housing developments indicates a NIMBYism ("not in my backyard") sentiment that contradicts the need for housing diversity across the city. We must change the community narrative around affordable housing and more dense developments. The new Metro Council Ad Hoc Land Use Committee could become the platform to discuss, educate, and act on these very issues, providing the framework for how to have productive community input when debating land use and zoning policy. State legislators involved with the Kentucky Housing Task Force can also support Louisville Metro's efforts to review and change the land development code to create more housing diversity for all Louisvillians.

The arc for housing justice is long and supported by a committed community organized around the belief that housing is not only a human right, but the keystone for a healthy, wealthy Louisville. The community needs full participation to ensure everyone has access to a home.

Scan QR to access "About Louisville's Housing Needs: Finding the Political Will to Build"

REDRESSING WEALTH DISPARITIES CAUSED BY INSTITUTIONAL RACISM IN HOUSING

JOHN D. BORDERS, JR.
Attorney, Borders & Borders, PLC

In 2020, after the killings of Breonna Taylor, George Floyd, and Ahmaud Arbery, we experienced the largest protests for civil rights in American history. Countless people, corporations, and nonprofits vowed "never again" to turn a blind eye to racism. Many organizations apologized for past racist practices. Diversity, Equity and Inclusion (DEI) offices and posts popped up in schools and businesses. If we experienced a reckoning in understanding, however, the data around Black wealth since 2020 tells us we failed to experience a reckoning in practice.

As a real estate attorney, I was shocked to learn, mostly from The Color of Law by Richard Rothstein, how the real estate industry conspired with government (every level and every branch) to plunder Black wealth. Through redlining (designating Black neighborhoods as unsafe for investment), restrictive covenants (neighborhood restrictions allowing only white purchasers), steering (directing people to and away from certain neighborhoods based on race), under-appraising properties in Black neighborhoods, barring Blacks from becoming realtors, and intimidating Blacks who tried to move to white neighborhoods, my industry partnered with government to make sure that white people could own homes in safe, prosperous neighborhoods while Black people would remain renters, often in urban ghettos. And because homeownership is the most common path to wealth building, this guaranteed that the middle class would become almost entirely white.

Since 2020 and the COVID-19 pandemic, racial wealth disparities have increased throughout the country. The pandemic was also followed by rising interest rates and a historically diminished inventory of homes for sale. In competitive markets, those who lose out are those with the most to lose, ensuring that wealth disparities continue.

Today, households with a Black resident make up 13.6% of all households but hold only 4.7% of all wealth.[1] And the median wealth of households with Black residents is $24,520, compared to $250,400 for households with white residents. The majority of Americans create generational wealth through equity they build in their home, not from stocks and bonds. Keeping Black people out of homeownership opportunities also kept them out of wealth building, and that resonates today.

Because we've had a great rise in property values and a great decline in available homes since the pandemic, the market is more competitive than ever. And that means that people with wealth will win most contract bidding wars. Indeed, because of these conditions—along with higher interest rates—new purchases by Black homeowners dropped by 50% between 2021-2022.[2] Once again, it's a challenge for marginalized people to buy homes.

So, what can we do to redress the wealth disparities we have created in our community?

- **"Place-based" solutions: improving housing, school quality, transportation, parks, medical care, healthy food, libraries, and businesses in neighborhoods redlined out of affluence**
- **"Mobility" approaches: opening white and affluent neighborhoods to more Black residents, marketing directly to African Americans; making reasonable financing available; providing down payment assistance; building multi-family dwellings and apartments in white neighborhoods.**
- **"Race-targeted" programs: giving preferences for better housing opportunities to historically neglected populations; building financial literacy through Black-focused nonprofits.**
- **Down payment assistance programs, like the Affordable Housing Trust Fund and Kentucky Housing Corporation (KHC)**
- **Modifying zoning ordinances to require developers to set aside a higher percentage of units (both for rent and for sale) to low- and moderate-income applicants.**

Single-family zoning needs to be rethought,] so more houses (and multi-family buildings) can be built on smaller lots.

- **Tax lien sales (where the city sells delinquent tax bills to purchasers who then foreclose on a home if the homeowner doesn't pay the bill and penalties) should be banned in historically redlined neighborhoods or, perhaps, limited to nonprofits to purchase the bills.**
- **White buyers and sellers can hire National Association of Real Estate Brokers (NAREB) realtors when they buy and sell houses. The organization was created in 1947 when Blacks were not allowed to be called realtors, and it continues today to promote and facilitate homeownership opportunities for African Americans.**
- **Support nonprofit builders like Habitat for Humanity, REBOUND, and River City Housing in their work to reverse the damage done by redlining. Volunteer with organizations like New Directions and Habitat for Humanity to help make home repairs in blighted neighborhoods.**
- **Landlords can stop asking tenants whether they were ever arrested or convicted of non-violent crimes.**
- **Contact your Congressperson to support H.R.40, creating a commission to study reparations for descendants of former slaves.**
- **Encourage your local and state representatives to make funding for affordable housing a greater priority.**

- **Encourage your local government to dedicate publicly owned land (parking lots, unused school buildings, tax-adjudicated properties, etc.) to affordable housing development.**

- **Encourage your local representatives to limit short-term rentals in neighborhoods with homes that would otherwise be affordable.**

- **Contact your local representative to encourage targeted infrastructure investments in previously-redlined neighborhoods rather than in affluent areas only.**

- **Implement right to counsel programs to provide pro bono attorneys to represent indigent tenants so they can raise defenses to evictions.**

The solutions aren't easy to implement, but neither are they impossible. Racial segregation was wrong, intentional, harmful to Black people, illegal, and anti-democratic. Together, as a community, we can begin to tear down barriers to homeownership and start to remedy the damage done by centuries of racist practices designed to keep African Americans from building wealth. Together, we can build a more equitable society. It starts with homeownership, and the building of generational wealth.

THE FAIR HOUSING ACT IS NOT WORKING

NATALIE HARRIS
Coalition for the Homeless

According to the U.S. Department of Justice, "One of the central objectives of the Fair Housing Act, when Congress enacted it in 1968, was to prohibit race discrimination in sales and rentals of housing."[1]

Unfortunately, it is not working.

When the Fair Housing Act passed in 1968, there was a 27% gap between Black and white homeownership. Over 50 years later, according to the National Association of Realtors' 2024 report "A Snapshot of Race and Home Buying in America," the overall homeownership rate in America has increased while the Black-white homeownership gap has also increased to 29% — with 73% of white households owning their homes and only 44% of Black households owning theirs.[2] The disparity is even greater in the Louisville Metro MSA where, in 2021, 40% of Black households owned their homes while the white homeownership rate was 70%.[3]

Page 86 Photo: REBOUND homes built in the Russell neighborhood in partnership with Russell: A Place of Promise

It is not because Black families have not used the Fair Housing Act to make their case. The Justice Department reports that the majority of fair housing claims over the past 30 years have been claims of race discrimination, even though many renters and homeowners may never know they are victims due to steering and false information.[4]

It is easy to see this discrimination on the local level. Between 2021 and 2023, 1,300 units of housing were denied zoning or site plan approval because prospective residents were expected to be Black. Further, Home Mortgage Disclosure Act data for Louisville Metro shows that in 2020, Black households made up only 8.4% of mortgage applications and only 7.6% of the loans originated.[5]

Even when Black households become homeowners, the U.S. Census shows that the opportunity for wealth gain is not equal. Fifty percent of all Black homeowners in Metro Louisville are located in 22 census tracts that saw little increase in value or, in some cases, a decrease from 2017 to 2021. Furthermore, Black property owners are five times more likely to lose their property due to eminent domain or other legal action.

So, why do we continue to expect the existing policies, including the Fair Housing Act, to make things right for Black households who have been losing wealth and opportunity for over 50 years? The answer is not to make things "fair" or "equal."

We need much stronger targeting of resources and prioritization of Black households if we are ever to address the decades of compounding inequity and discrimination they have faced. And, most importantly, targeted programs that work to address disparities created by America's history of systemic racism are not discriminatory; they are anti-discriminatory.

- **We need more programs like Louisville's REVERT Program that will provide up to $50,000 each to 216 households disproportionately impacted by redlining in previously redlined neighborhoods.**
- **We need down payment assistance to make homeownership a reality for Black households in all areas of Louisville Metro.**
- **We need repair funds targeted to families in homes that have not increased in value so that these important units and longtime residents are not lost in our city's previously redlined neighborhoods.**
- **And, perhaps most of all, we need greater oversight of programs that are meant to target low-income citizens, yet never get to those in the greatest need.**

The existing laws created to protect the rights of housing and wealth building for Black citizens are not working. Let's focus on responses that do.

BLACK BUSINESS

"

IN 2022, **BLACK BUSINESSES** WERE ROUGHLY **THREE TIMES MORE LIKELY** TO GET **REJECTED** FOR A BANK LOAN VERSUS WHITE BUSINESSES, **EVEN WITH** SEVERAL ACCELERATOR PROGRAMS RUNNING AT THAT TIME.

DANA J. JOHNSON

"

ACCELERATORS ARE NOT ENOUGH TO ADDRESS BLACK WEALTH DISPARITIES

DANA J. JOHNSON
Senior Director, Diversity, Equity, and Inclusion
Greater Louisville Inc. — The Metro Chamber of Commerce

Louisville used to be known as "The Harlem of the South," bustling with Black businesses on Old Walnut Street — the city's hub for Black businesses during segregation. Despite Old Walnut Street's cultural and social importance to Black businesses, it was eventually demolished, and many Black businesses disappeared, eliminating Black prosperity in the city. Recently, many organizations have started accelerator programs to strengthen the city's Black business core. While those programs have been helpful in many ways, they cannot fully address the primary barriers that keep Black businesses from starting and growing in our city: accessing funding. Without access to funds, Louisville's Black business scene will struggle to survive.

Louisville's business leaders have worked to address this problem through educational business "accelerator" programs designed to help them either start-up or expand their growth and reach. These programs vary in scope and intensity, but they all have the same mission: to equip Black entrepreneurs with the necessary resources, skills, and knowledge to compete in Kentucky. While these programs provide many benefits to Black businesses, they alone cannot solve the problem entrepreneurs have accessing capital to scale their ventures.

Many Black business owners are unable to secure grants or loans, and banks often demand extensive collateral before approving them. In 2022, Black businesses were roughly three times more likely to get rejected for a bank loan versus white businesses,[1] even with several accelerator programs running at that time. As a result, Black entrepreneurs still find themselves cashing out their 401(k)s to fund their businesses. When coupled with the fact that many Black entrepreneurs do not have access to the necessary resources and networks needed to confidently pursue certain types of funding due to systemic racism and discrimination, the path toward funding a Black business is rocky. This is where incubator and accelerator programs come in.

The idea is that those programs are meant to plug the gaps in wealth disparities in the city by providing the knowledge and resources to acquire funding. While this may be happening in some accelerators, it is clearly not enough to increase Louisville's 2% Black business ownership statistic.

Today, Black business ownership is still around 2-3% and is not drastically improving, even with help from incubator and accelerator fund assistance. Even more so, in 2022, Black-owned businesses had around a 50% chance of failing within five years. This can be attributed to a lack of venture capital to get them off the ground and keep them around, on top of a lack of funding for marketing that incubator programs are not able to fully provide. While Louisville's accelerator programs are making strides, we need additional support from our government partners to remove barriers and provide new resources. We hear a lot about what the government does to uplift Black businesses, but that effort is not reflected in the realities Black entrepreneurs still face in 2024.

Given the aforementioned issues, incubator and accelerator programs are not enough on their own to help Black businesses in the city. We need the support of both our business community and local and state governments to lead the charge. The government can lean in and provide a comprehensive list of the city's fund assistance programs and what they offer. The government can also directly fund accelerator programs rather than having them rely on the generosity of corporate investors.

Local governments should proactively establish partnerships with underrepresented business owners to increase access to public contracts, procurement opportunities, and other business opportunities. This means resources and mentorship programs to support start-ups and other enterprises should be developed and funded.

Lenders and investors that help provide economic opportunity and financial stability to underrepresented areas should be supported and incentivized.

Accelerator program leaders should emphasize funding access and contract securement in their program curriculum. They should work more closely together to share funding opportunities everyone can benefit from. Accelerator program leaders should also consider giving entrepreneurs opportunities to speak to the city's buyers and investors.

By taking these steps, Louisville can start addressing systemic barriers to funding and create a more equitable and inclusive future where Black-owned businesses thrive and contribute to the city's economy — and Louisville can once again become "The Harlem of the South."

LOUISVILLE MUST GROW OUR ECONOMY THROUGH EDUCATION, EMPHASIZING BUSINESS OPPORTUNITIES AND FUTURE WORKFORCE

DELQUAN DORSEY
Supplier Diversity and Community Engagement Coordinator of JCPS

"In 1969, Black people made up 13.3% of Jefferson County's population, but owned 4.6% of the county's businesses. Today, although the Black population has grown — to 22.4% — its ownership of businesses with employees is 2.4%. That mark places the city last out of 16 peer cities, according to Greater Louisville Inc. Nationally, based on 2017 census data, 2.2% of businesses are Black-owned, while Black people make up 13% of the country's population."

Hayes Gardner—Louisville Courier-Journal, Dec. 14, 2020; updated Dec. 22, 2020 [1]

Echoing Hayes Gardner's article, the African American population growth in Louisville is not in line with the growth and sustainability of our businesses. Several historical factors have caused this dismal economic situation for African Americans locally and nationally. Since Reconstruction, there has not been a sustained effort by the powers-that-be — namely government officials and philanthropists — to economically address the tremendous sacrifice the descendants of enslaved Africans made to allow a small percentage of wealthy Americans to thrive. As a result, the Black community still struggles to access the economic opportunities that would change their quality of life in this country. This lack of economic growth continues to impact outcomes in education. We know that when families are better off economically, the children often experience more success academically. The current attack on Diversity, Equity, and Inclusion (DEI) efforts is another example of the rich and powerful's efforts to re-establish the barriers that make Black people consumers who never really benefit as producers.

In order to thrive and grow as a functioning economy and community, Black and Brown families must become producers. To meet this challenge, students must be more than employable; they must be prepared to own businesses that create even more jobs. The majority of jobs come from small businesses. If the broader professional community will work more intentionally with JCPS, we can create pipelines that lead to a more robust local economy of young people ready to own businesses that make Louisville and the Commonwealth of Kentucky economically relevant. We also know that when this local landscape is blossoming with talent and skills, it creates more tax revenue for local government and the school district.

How do we realize this vision of a blossoming landscape full of African American producers?

Public organizations and private companies must commit to continuing DEI programs like supplier diversity programs that focus on doing business with minority and women Business enterprises. In my role as the Supplier Diversity Coordinator for Jefferson County Public Schools (JCPS), I represent the school district on Mayor Greenberg's Equity in Contracting & Procurement Task Force. This task force is made up of more than ten local, public-governmental organizations that focus on their inclusion of minority-owned businesses in construction and renovation contracts. Many of the organizations on the task force understand the importance of mentorship and exposure to opportunities, so they engage JCPS students at career fairs and job shadowing experiences at their company work sites.

We need private companies to follow the model of this task force. If private companies (large and small in scale) all focused on inclusion and intentionally creating space for Black and Brown business owners and professionals, we would reap the benefits. Organizations in the African American community would need less philanthropic support because companies from the African American community would fill that philanthropic role. I once heard it said that if the Black community had more economic opportunities, then we wouldn't need as many grants and handouts.

What we need is for more professionals of all backgrounds (especially African Americans) to connect Black and Brown students to mentorship and money-making opportunities within their industry, trade, and profession. Our young people today are not satisfied with the "high school to college to good job" formula that was laid out for my generation. Now more than ever, there is a challenge to connect some of the traditional content taught in school with income opportunities in the current workforce. Since professionals have made the journey of education to career, we should demonstrate how education and training lead to well-paid professions by providing more internships and co-op experiences. Some of the complaints I hear in the business community are "We can't find qualified people to work," and "Nobody wants to work." While these sentiments may be the impact of the COVID-19 pandemic on our workforce and economy, complaint without solution will not change these results.

Life is too short to just throw up our hands and blame others. **Let's do all we can to open our minds, execute new strategies, and celebrate the current efforts to educate and develop our future and existing workforce.**

INVESTING IN THE FUTURE OF BLACK BUSINESS

CYNTHIA BROWN
Director, Center for Entrepreneurship
Louisville Urban League

In 2020, the pandemic and social unrest pulled back the covers and exposed the realities of the full impact of racial disparities. But we always knew they were there. The only thing new was the inability to continue ignoring it. For Black businesses across the US, that reality was stark. Yes, all small businesses struggled, but even when help was supposed to be on the way, many Black businesses were less likely to receive grants or were unable to access recovery funds. Black businesses that were already financially fragile were closing at twice the rate of their white counterparts, with a staggering 41% closing their doors for good.[1] At the time, Louisville actually fared a bit worse than national statistics. Despite its population being almost 23% Black, just over 2% of businesses were Black-owned.[2]

As a result, the events of 2020 spurred a flurry of activity. Numerous incubators, accelerators, and technical assistance programs started. Capital providers began to focus on new initiatives that were intentional about inclusive access. Born out of the work of A Path Forward,[3] the Louisville Urban League created its own Center for Entrepreneurship. Since 2020, the ecosystem of resources has grown, and partners have worked in collaboration to create networks of support for Black businesses. Hundreds of budding entrepreneurs have enrolled in programs and started their journeys to being Black business owners.

Yet, in 2024, the numbers have not significantly increased — especially when it comes to employer businesses. The pool of established businesses with the highest growth potential was decimated during the pandemic. So while we have seen increases in new businesses and more program support, we are only making up lost ground.

In the past year, we have seen a rise in anti-diversity efforts, and the business space has not been exempt. We've seen lawsuits targeting funds aimed at minority and women-owned businesses and even challenges against the Small Business Administration's 8(a) program. Organizations in both the philanthropic and corporate sectors are now second-guessing support for race-based initiatives, fearing possible litigation. However, support for Black-owned businesses cannot be a passing fad or put on the back burner out of fear. The investment must be long-term and promote sustainable strategies, or everybody loses.

A 2020 Brookings study projected, "If the number of Black businesses matched the population size and the revenue of each of those firms matched non-Black businesses' revenue, then the total revenue of Black businesses would increase by $5.9

trillion."[4] Increasing and growing Black businesses has the potential to impact local economies significantly. The new system must be supported to continue the work that has been started if we are to make any progress toward parity.

Two core pieces are needed to ensure the success of Black businesses. Black businesses need access to capital, which includes traditional amortizing business loans, grants, non-traditional funding, and equity investment. Black businesses need to have capital options that are flexible and responsive to particular challenges to enable businesses to get out of survival mode and into business growth. However, access to capital on its own is not enough. Black businesses need technical assistance that incorporates a network of providers who can advise, coach, strategically plan, educate, and connect resources.

Beyond these two core pieces, a comprehensive network of mentoring, revenue generation opportunities, innovation strategies, and professional development is needed to address the systemic barriers that have historically impeded the development of Black businesses. A combination of private and public partnerships must be achieved for consistent investments to ensure that these developing networks of resources stay sustainable.

In addition to home ownership, thriving businesses have always been a cornerstone of flourishing communities — especially Black communities. We see this from Tulsa's Black Wall Street to Louisville's own Old Walnut Street in the Russell neighborhood. Business ownership has long been one of the primary ways to establish financial stability and the creation of wealth. The 2019 Survey of Consumer Finances indicates that Black families have eight times less wealth than typical white families.[5] A city can't be truly successful with this large of a wealth gap where almost a quarter of its population struggles to access the pathway of prosperity through business.

Invest in the future of Black businesses. Can we really afford not to?

THE IMPORTANCE OF ECONOMIC POWER IN THE BLACK COMMUNITY

DAVE W. CHRISTOPHER, SR.
President & Founder, Amped

It really is about money. Blacks have been at the bottom of the wealth gap since the 1980s, when the Pew Research Center began tracking wealth gap data. The belief has been that if we worked harder, got more education, and owned homes, we would all be better off and that the wealth gap between Black and white households would narrow. Although these directives have merit, they are not the sole solutions. How can we obtain these things that will assure economic power?

It takes money to make money, but where does the money come from? We are locked out of the workplaces where the jobs pay at or above a thriving wage. We are locked out of the banks that provide access to fair capital to operate a successful business. We are locked out of access to home loans to purchase homes in neighborhoods of our choosing that will grow in value over time.

My solution is economic power– a community's access to wealth and ability to improve its living standards. History has proven that the wealth gap will either remain the same or get worse without economic power for the whole community and not just for a few.

Amped is dedicated to building the community's economic power by getting its participants, both young and old, to completion and self-sustainability. Each of our programs is focused on building economic power in underserved communities with a particular focus on underserved Black communities. In our music program, the students are encouraged to learn every aspect of the music industry. When they learn their craft and are asked to create or perform using the skills that they learn at Amped, we encourage them to charge a fee for their services or performances. We teach them that their work has value. We emphasize to them that they need to begin generating wealth early. The Amped Russell Technology Business Incubator is a year-long business incubator for Black and Brown businesses that provides all that the businesses need to be profitable and create generational wealth. The Amped Technology Workforce Development program is a twelve-week intensive program that not only trains and certifies our participants but connects them directly to employers to interview for jobs in technology that begin at or above a thriving wage. Amped understands that it really is about the money. We cannot continue to pretend that it is not.

In 2015, a year after Amped was founded Louisville Metro Parks leased one of their underused buildings so that we could expand our music program. In that same year and following years Amped received funding and volunteer support from public and private foundations and corporations such as Metro United Way, Fund For The Arts, Brown Forman, Humana, YUM Brands, Louisville Urban League, and so many others. I believe that putting money in the pockets of Black people through jobs in technology that start at a thriving wage as well as providing sufficient amounts of fair capital that will allow Black businesses to thrive and grow can move us in the right direction. Governments, corporations, foundations, individuals, and nonprofits need to support access to capital in communities so that we can build economic power.

FURTHER REFLECTIONS

A DEMONSTRATION OF PHILANTHROPY AND BLACK COMMUNITIES AS STRATEGIC PARTNERS AND CHAMPIONS FOR TRANSFORMATIVE CHANGE

RAMONA DALLUM
Senior Vice President,
Community Leadership
Community Foundation of Louisville

The Community Foundation of Louisville recognizes that access and absorption of financial capital is a primary determinant for accelerating and sustaining transformative change. Within the past 10 years, several scholars including Edgar Villanueva *(Decolonizing Wealth: Indigenous Wisdom to Heal Divides and Restore Balance)*, Isabel Wilkerson *(Caste: The Origins of Our Discontents)*, and Heather McGhee *(The Sum of Us: What Racism Costs All of Us and How We Can Prosper Together)* describe systems that intentionally create barriers to financial capital for many communities, especially Black and Indigenous populations.

Philanthropy has played a role in sustaining practices that have made accessing capital more difficult for historically low-wealth and overlooked communities. In her essay, ***"The Conviction to Champion Equity: Philanthropy's Role in Empowering Leaders of Color",*** Adria Johnson discusses data related to philanthropic investment in Black communities. After seeing similar data in 2017, the Community Foundation of Louisville began to assess our behavior and its impact on low-wealth communities candidly. After the senseless police killing of Breonna Taylor and COVID-19's spotlight on race-based, quality-of-life disparities, the Foundation re-committed to understanding our role in creating barriers to financial capital. This commitment is rooted in the values and practices of Trust-Based Philanthropy, an approach that encourages the redistribution of power in the non-profit sector.

Communities are identified as low wealth based on their residents' level of accumulated financial capital. However, there is extraordinary wealth in communities with this label. These communities are wealthy in innovation, creativity, intellect, passion, and commitment. Leaders of local nonprofit organizations like River City Drum Corps Cultural Arts Institute, Play Cousins Collective, Bridge Kids International, and No More Red Dots have impacted the quality of life for people living in low-wealth communities. They have done this with extremely limited access to financial capital. These organizations, and others like them, have been expected to prove their worthiness to receive philanthropic capital by conforming their leadership, governance, and evaluation practices to align with the historical practices of the philanthropic sector.

The Community Foundation of Louisville is committed to creating new systems that rely on the greatest assets of low-wealth communities: its people.

Over the past four years, we have embarked on a learning journey with leaders of Black-led and Black-serving institutions to create new practices for accessing financial capital. We have worked with Black leaders to: share decision-making for our grantmaking; identify gaps in the Black business ecosystem; cultivate a pipeline of Black founders; convene to develop a strategy for accessing federal dollars; and develop tools for accessing transformative capital for affordable housing, job creation, and land development. During this time, most of our capital has been provided as unrestricted operating support.

Black leaders have shared with us that these unrestricted dollars have provided them with the autonomy to determine the most meaningful use of resources. The providing of these unrestricted dollars has also demonstrated the Foundation's respect for their expertise, leadership, and lived experience. Most of Louisville's Black-led, nonprofit organizations are led by college-educated people, many with master's and doctoral credentials. Assuming these leaders are incapable of the financial management of their organizations is insulting and degrading. During our time walking alongside these leaders, we have learned that providing the infrastructure to help them reflect on their practices and identify their unique measures of success is as important as financial capital.

Traditionally, foundations invest 95% of their philanthropic assets in the stock market for a return on investment. The remaining 5% is generally used for grantmaking that provides dollars for charitable programs. Black leaders challenged us to unlock this 95% of our philanthropic capital in the form of below-market-rate loans, lines of credit, loan guarantees, and equities. In response to this call, the Community Foundation of Louisville launched Invest Louisville in July 2024. Invest Louisville is an investment option that allows Foundation fundholders and others to invest an allocation of their philanthropic assets in local projects. [1] These investments, which focus on affordable housing, job creation, and land development, will have a targeted return on investment of 3% and an even greater impact on the quality of life for all Louisville residents.

Invest Louisville will provide a mechanism to activate the 95% for local benefit by providing favorable debt and continuing to fund grants. Through Invest Louisville, the Foundation aims, over several years, to activate a network of community-focused individuals, foundations, and corporations to make $100 million in philanthropic capitalavailable to overlooked communities at below-market terms. This alone will not close Louisville's $250 million philanthropic need identified by "A Path Forward",[2] but it is a start toward disrupting harmful systems.

Systems designed to restrict access to financial capital have worked successfully for centuries. Creating culturally appropriate and inclusive capital access systems require patience, ingenuity, experimentation, and failing forward. The seven universal principles necessary for thriving communities are unity, self-determination, collective work and responsibility, cooperative economics, purpose, creativity, and faith. Together, philanthropy and Black leaders of community-based organizations can actively embrace these values. We can be strategic partners and champions for transformative change. By accepting our shared responsibility for the collective work, we can usher in a movement where all Louisville residents can absorb financial capital to support self-determination. We must hold each other accountable for realizing this vision.

THE CONVICTION TO CHAMPION EQUITY: PHILANTHROPY'S ROLE IN EMPOWERING LEADERS OF COLOR METRO UNITED WAY

ADRIA JOHNSON
President and CEO of Metro United Way

In the face of one of the most divisive and formidable periods in our recent history, the imperative for leaders of color to be steadfast in our convictions, uphold our values, and relentlessly pursue equity has become increasingly critical. Metro United Way, in partnership with the Louisville Urban League and its six pillars of action — Jobs, Justice, Education, Health, Housing, and Black Business — recognizes the pivotal role philanthropy must play in empowering all Black leaders to realize their transformative potential.

According to research by the Center for American Progress, increasing the economic participation and leadership of Black communities can lead to substantial GDP growth. Specifically, if the racial wealth gap between Black and white households were closed, the U.S. economy could see a potential increase of $1.5 trillion to $2.1 trillion in GDP annually.[1] This highlights the critical importance of investing in Black-led social change initiatives to unlock economic potential and create a more equitable society.

Philanthropic engagement in Black Louisville transcends mere charity; it represents a strategic and ethical obligation to address the systemic disparities that have long impeded the progress of the Black community. Through strategic and intentional philanthropy, we can dismantle barriers and forge opportunities that allow leaders to govern with conviction and champion the cause of justice.

For philanthropic entities to effectuate their role, they must adopt a proactive, deliberate stance that includes the following strategies:

1. **Empower leaders of color by offering leadership development programs, mentorship, and platforms to elevate their voices and perspectives**

2. **Support community-led initiatives that confront the distinct challenges of Black Louisville, such as economic empowerment, equitable access to quality education, and healthcare equity**

3. **Foster collaborations that bridge the divide among diverse communities and stakeholders, encouraging dialogue and empathy**

4. Ensure accountability by tracking the impact of philanthropic endeavors on the progression of equity and justice

Philanthropy's role in this mission must be marked by both the extent of our investments and the depth of our engagement. The call for solidarity is unequivocal, and the time for action is now. Together, we can redefine Louisville not by its disparities, but by its commitment to justice, opportunity, and inclusivity. As we delve deeper into the significance of philanthropic investment in Black Louisville, there are innovative strategies and models that have surfaced recently, advocating for sustainable change.

The Black L.O.V.E. (Live, Own, Vote, Excel) model, in the form of a statistical algorithm and derived from comprehensive research, introduces a novel, econometric model to evaluate the economic distress faced by those at risk of unemployment and rising living costs.[2] We ask ourselves, "How can we quantify the need for increased investment in Black-led, social change initiatives that not only meets immediate needs, but also promotes intergenerational community wealth building?"

Our analysis of Black L.O.V.E. philanthropy in Louisville, utilizing data from 2003-2020, reveals that targeting the Black community's needs in areas aligned with the L.O.V.E. dimensions — Living, Owning, Voting, and Excelling — comprise less than 2% of all grants to Louisville communities during this period.[3] This stark statistic underscores the necessity for a deliberate shift in funding priorities.

LOUISVILLE GRANTS 2003 - 2020

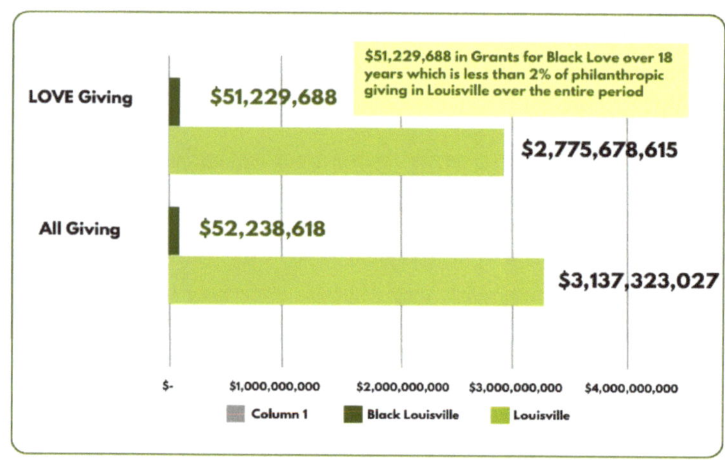

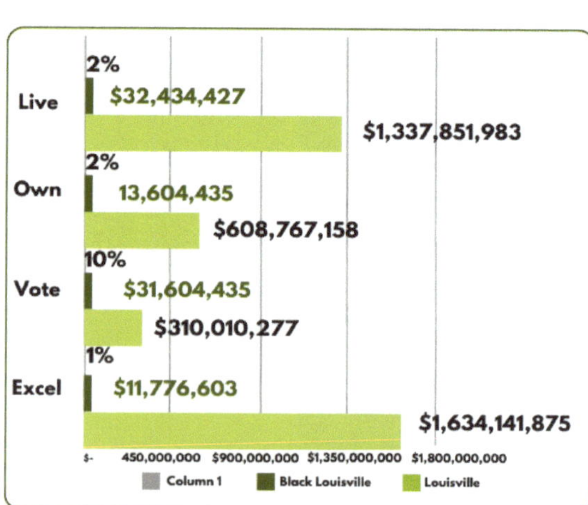

Data taken from Candid © 2021 Candid

By integrating philanthropic data with insights from local authorities and community voices, we can identify targeted interventions and strategic collaborations. This united approach not only amplifies the effect of philanthropic efforts, but also sets the stage for enduring, generational change.

Our Black L.O.V.E. Philanthropic Partnership (BLPP) not only has the capacity to raise and distribute funds for these priorities, but can also facilitate meaningful funding relationships between major donors and grassroots groups within Greater Louisville's Black communities. Additionally, it seeks to enhance the capacity of funders with limited corporate responsibility or philanthropic staff to invest in and evaluate Black L.O.V.E. outcomes.

By leveraging the transformative potential of philanthropy and utilizing data-driven strategies, we pave the way for a future where Black leaders are empowered, communities are uplifted, and the pursuit of equity and justice becomes an attainable reality.

We issue a rallying cry to every community stakeholder. We must be bold in our pursuit of equity, strategic in our approach, and steadfast in our support for the leaders who are the standard-bearers of change. Let us invest with purpose, advocate with passion, and stand united in solidarity. For it is only through our collective efforts that we can transform the landscape of opportunity for Black Louisville — all of Louisville — and create a more just and equitable community for all.

THE BLACK PATHWAY FORWARD

BEYOND THE NOW

Crisis Investing

Civil unrest related to two high profile police shootings, and subsequent protests raised the awareness of the important role philanthropic investment plays in funding change we believe in

TO THE ONGOING JOURNEY

Learning to apply the BLPP Frame to philanthropic investing

The BLPP Framework for increasing capacity in the Louisville community id one that once learned, adopted and scaled will become a system for sustainable change

THE NEAR TERM GROWTH

Elevating the standard of investment in community with philanthropic partnerships

The cohort model within BLPP fosters the ability to build and strengthen relationships within the non-profit + philanthropic sector to form a system needed to support growth and advancement

THE LONG TERM ADVANCEMENT

Building a sustainable business model for transformative change

The BLPP as it continues to mature and grow will deepen its ability to serve as the connector between Black led organizations committed to solutions driven pursuits and funders who share their vision

ENDNOTES

It's Always Halloween

1 The Pew Charitable Trusts. (2023, May 16). Racial disparities persist in many U.S. jails: Despite narrowed gap in incarceration rates, Black people remain overrepresented in jail populations, admissions — and stay longer on average. https://www.pewtrusts.org/en/research-and-analysis/issue-briefs/2023/05/racial-disparities-persist-in-many-us-jails

2 American Civil Liberties Union. (n.d.). Race and Criminal Justice. https://www.aclu.org/issues/racial-justice/race-and-criminal-justice

3 CBS 8 San Diego. (2021, February 17). Racial disparities in the criminal justice system [Video]. YouTube. https://www.youtube.com/watch?app=desktop&v=9PNNAUrFiA8

4 CBS 8 San Diego. (2021, February 17). Racial disparities in the criminal justice system [Video]. YouTube. https://www.youtube.com/watch?app=desktop&v=9PNNAUrFiA8

5 U.S. Office of Juvenile Justice and Delinquency Prevention. (2014, November). Literature review: Disproportionate Minority Contact (DMC). https://ojjdp.ojp.gov/mpg/literature-review/disproportionate-minority-contact.pdf

6 Wilson, V., & Darity Jr., W. (2022, March 25). Understanding black-white disparities in labor market outcomes requires models that account for persistent discrimination and unequal bargaining power. Economic Policy Institute. https://www.epi.org/unequalpower/publications/understanding-black-white-disparities-in-labor-market-outcomes/

7 Bhutta, N., Hizmo, A., & Ringo, D. (2022). How much does racial bias affect mortgage lending? Evidence from human algorithmic credit decisions. Board of Governors of the Federal Reserve System. https://www.federalreserve.gov/econres/feds/files/2022067pap.pdf

8 Morales-Doyle, S., & Karalunas, L.M. (2024, August 22). Project 2025's anti-voter agenda. Brennan Center. https://www.brennancenter.org/our-work/research-reports/project-2025s-anti-voter-agenda

9 Perera, R.M., Valant, J., & Meyer, K. (2024, August 12). Project 2025 and education: A lot of bad ideas, some more actionable than others. The Brookings Institution. https://www.brookings.edu/articles/project-2025-and-education-a-lot-of-bad-ideas-some-more-actionable-than-others/

JOBS

Investment in Black Workers is Critical to Construction Workforce

1 Biu, O., Katz, B., Adu-Gyamfi, A., Scott, M. (2023, September). Job quality and race and gender equity: Understanding the link between job quality and occupational crowding. Urban Institute. https://www.urban.org/sites/default/files/2023-09/Job-quality-and-race-and-gender-equity.pdf

2 Biu, O., Katz, B., Adu-Gyamfi, A., Scott, M. (2023, September). Job quality and race and gender equity: Understanding the link between job quality and occupational crowding. Urban Institute.

https://www.urban.org/sites/default/files/2023-09/Job-quality-and-race-and-gender-equity.pdf

A Housing Crisis Masquerading as a Workforce Problem

1 National Housing Conference. (n.d.). *Effective employer-assisted housing programs.* https://nhc.org/policy-guide/employer-assisted-housing-the-basics/effective-employer-assisted-housing-programs/

2 Metropolitan Housing Coalition. (2020). *Analysis of impediments to fair housing choice in Louisville Metro, KY.* Louisville Metro Department of Housing and Family Services. https://metropolitanhousing.org/wp-content/uploads/2020/10/FINAL_2020-AI_MHC_May-11-2020.pdf

3 Shroyer, A., & Gaitán, V. (2019, September 11). *Four reasons why employers should care about housing.* Housing Matters. https://housingmatters.urban.org/articles/four-reasons-why-employers-should-care-about-housing

4 National Governors Association. (2023, May 11). *How governors are addressing housing access and affordability and the connection to workforce success.* https://www.nga.org/news/commentary/how-governors-are-addressing-housing-access-and-affordability-and-the-connection-to-workforce-success/

JUSTICE

The More Things Change

1 Kentucky General Assembly. (n.d.) *Constitution of Kentucky (Includes amendments ratified on or before November 5, 2024).* https://apps.legislature.ky.gov/law/constitution

2 *New International Bible.* (2011). Zondervan. (Original work published 1978)

3 *New International Bible.* (2011). Zondervan. (Original work published 1978)

The 2024 Legislative Session and the State of Black Louisville

1 Office of State Budget Director. (2021). *Kentucky general fund receipts analysis.* Commonwealth of Kentucky. https://osbd.ky.gov/

2 Office of State Budget Director. (2021). *Kentucky general fund receipts analysis.* Commonwealth of Kentucky. https://osbd.ky.gov/

3 Sayer, R. (2023, September 22). U.S. Education Sec.: Law violated by Underfunding Kentucky State University, other hbcus. *LEX 18 News.* https://www.lex18.com/news/u-s-education-sec-law-violated-by-underfunding-kentucky-state-university-other-hbcus

4 Horsley, M. (2024, June 5). Kentucky State University officials brief lawmakers on progress since 2022 bailout. *Kentucky Lantern.* https://kentuckylantern.com/2024/06/05/kentucky-state-university-officials-brief-lawmakers-on-progress-since-2022-bailout/

5 Kentucky Cabinet for Health and Family Services. (2021). *Public health maternal mortality review: A report of data from years 2013-2019.* https://www.chfs.ky.gov/agencies/dph/dmch/Documents/MMRAnnualReport.pdf

6 March of Dimes Peristats. (February 2024). *Mortality and morbidity.* https://www.marchofdimes.org/peristats/data?reg=99&top=6&stop=92&lev=1&slev=4&obj=1&sreg=21

7 Thomas, P., Raymer, K., Bailey, J., & Spalding, A. (2024, February 27). *House Bill 5 would cost Kentucky more than $1 billion over a decade.* Kentucky Center for Economic Policy. https://kypolicy.org/house-bill-5-would-cost-kentucky-more-than-1-billion-over-the-next-decade/

8 Thomas, P., Raymer, K., Bailey, J., & Spalding, A. (2024, February 27). *House Bill 5 would cost Kentucky more than $1 billion over a decade.* Kentucky Center for Economic Policy. https://kypolicy.org/house-bill-5-would-cost-kentucky-more-than-1-billion-over-the-next-decade/

9 Bennet, J. (2024, March 4). *As GOP pushes Safer Kentucky Act, full jails prep for more crowds.* Louisville Public Media. https://www.lpm.org/investigate/2024-03-04/as-gop-pushes-safer-kentucky-act-full-jails-prep-for-more-crowds

10 Kentucky Youth Advocates. (2023). *County Data Book.* https://kyyouth.org/wp-content/uploads/2023/11/2023-County-Data-Book.pdf

11 National Council on Family Relations. (January 2018). How parental incarceration harms children and what to do about it. https://www.hindahelps.com/media/pdf/1218/NcYj12184061.pdf

12 U.S. Department of Justice. (March 2021). Parents in prison and their minor children. https://bjs.ojp.gov/content/pub/pdf/pptmcspi16st.pdf

13 Blueprint for Kentucky's Children. (December 2020). Data trends and policy recommendations to address the impact of maternal incarceration on Kentucky's children. https://kyyouth.org/wp-content/uploads/2020/12/BlueprintBrief_ParentalIncarceration_Dec2020.pdf

14 Prison Policy Initiative. (n.d.). Kentucky profile. https://www.prisonpolicy.org/profiles/KY.html#:~:text=Kentucky%20incarcerates%20women%20at%20a,an%20hour%20for%20their%20work

When Injustice Becomes Law, Rebellion Becomes Duty: How Coalition Building is Necessary to Sustain Our Commonwealth

1 Townsend, B. (2024, February 19). Kentucky legislators have introduced 14 anti-LGBTQ+ bills: Here's what to know. Queer Kentucky. https://queerkentucky.com/kentucky-legislators-have-introduced-14-anti-lgbtq-bills-heres-what-to-know/

2 Townsend, B. (2024, February 19). Kentucky legislators have introduced 14 anti-LGBTQ+ bills: Here's what to know. Queer Kentucky. https://queerkentucky.com/kentucky-legislators-have-introduced-14-anti-lgbtq-bills-heres-what-to-know/

3 Clark, J. (2024, February 8). Anti-DEI bill targeting higher education clears Kentucky Senate Committee. Louisville Public Media. https://www.lpm.org/news/2024-02-08/anti-dei-bill-targeting-higher-education-clears-kentucky-senate-committee

4 Townsend, B. (2024, February 19). Kentucky legislators have introduced 14 anti-LGBTQ+ bills: Here's what to know. Queer Kentucky. https://queerkentucky.com/kentucky-legislators-have-introduced-14-anti-lgbtq-bills-heres-what-to-know/

5 Fairness Campaign. (n.d.). About us. https://www.fairness.org/about-us/

Key Takeaways From the History of Policing in Louisville: A Fact-Finding Report on Institutional Harms

1 Jamison, F., Issar, S., Fosl, C., Todd, M., Gorton, E., & Johnson, I. (2024). The History of Policing in Louisville: A Fact-Finding Report on Institutional Harms.

The State of White Allyship in Black Louisville

1 Wright, G.C. (2004). Life behind a veil: Blacks in Louisville, Kentucky, 1865-1930. LSU Press.

2 Wright, G.C. (2004). Life behind a veil: Blacks in Louisville, Kentucky, 1865-1930. LSU Press.

3 Weekly, F. (2023, August 23). Addressing the racial homeownership gap in Louisville. Federal Reserve Bank of St. Louis. https://www.stlouisfed.org/publications/bridges/2023/vol3/addressing-racial-homeownership-gap-louisville

4 Louisville Metro Government. (2023, December 22). Growing Louisville together. Louisville Metro Government Economic Development Plan. https://louisvilleky.gov/economic-development/document/growing-louisville-together-final-12-22-2023

5 Gardner, H. (2020, December 14). '200 Years behind': racial wealth gap impedes Black business ownership in Louisville. Courier Journal. https://www.courier-journal.com/in-depth/news/local/2020/12/14/black-louisville-business-owners-start-behind-due-to-wealth-gap/6507785002/

6 Rothwell, J., & Perry, A.M. (2021, November 17). Biased appraisals and the devaluation of housing in Black neighborhoods. The Brookings Institution. https://www.brookings.edu/articles/biased-appraisals-and-the-devaluation-of-housing-in-black-neighborhoods/

7 Nazgol, G., Barry, C., & Trinka, L. (2023, December 7). One in five: Racial disparity in imprisonment — causes and remedies. The Sentencing Project. https://www.sentencingproject.org/publications/one-in-five-racial-disparity-in-imprisonment-causes-and-remedies/

8 Ahebee, S. (2021, February 19). 'They see me as a role model': Black teachers improve education outcomes for Black students. The Pulse. https://whyy.org/segments/they-see-me-as-a-role-model-black-teachers-improve-education-outcomes-for-black-students/

A Path Forward for Louisville. (2020, June 19). https://apathforward4lou.org/

The Louisville Metro Police Department Must Do Better for Black People
1 United States Department of Justice Civil Rights Division, United States Attorney's Office Western District of Kentucky Civil Division. (2023, December 8). Investigation of the Louisville Metro Police Department and Louisville Metro Government. https://www.justice.gov/opa/press-release/file/1573011/download

2 Jamison, F., Issar, S., Fosl, C., Todd, M., Gorton, E., Johnson, I. (2024, January). The History of Policing in Louisville: A Fact-Finding Report on Institutional Harms. https://louisvilleky.gov/mayor-craig-greenberg/document/2024-history-policing-louisville?utm_medium=email&utm_source=govdelivery

3 Epley, K. (2021, August). The summer Louisville rose up: An examination of protest arrests June- September 2020. https://drive.google.com/file/d/1ZyrPKmRynwhTTRRE5c530Kh2Uv4TzY2e/view

4 Louisville Metropolitan Police Department. (n.d.). Information in reference to DOJ findings report. https://louisville-police.org/895/Information-in-Reference-to-DOJ-Findings?utm_medium=email&utm_source=govdelivery

5 Parrish-Wright, S. (2024, May 29). The People's Consent Decree resolution. Louisville Metro Council. https://content.govdelivery.com/bulletins/gd/KYLOUISVILLE-39f6755

EDUCATION

Future Focus of Racial Equity
1 Jefferson County Public Schools. (n.d.). Racial Equity Policy resource site. https://sites.google.com/jefferson.kyschools.us/jcpsracialequitypolicyhandbook

HBCUs are Imperative to Black Progress; They Need Financial Support From Liberal Allies
1 Mays, B.E. (1967, May 30). Twenty-seven years of success and failure at Morehouse College: Centennial Commencement Address 1967. Morehouse College Vertical Files. http://hdl.handle.net/20.500.12322/auc.141:0005

2 Clerkin , C., Dayal, S. , Mika, G., Sato, G., Speight, M., Wolcheck, D. (2023, May 2). Philanthropy and HBCUs: Foundation funding to historically Black colleges and universities. ABFE - A Philanthropic Partnership for Black Communities; Candid. https://www.issuelab.org/resources/41808/41808.pdf

3 Obernauer, C. (2023, July 5). Foundation funding Of HBCUs billions behind Ivy Leagues. The Non-profit Times. https://thenonprofittimes.com/foundations/foundation-funding-of-hbcus-billions-behind-ivy-leagues

4 Ma, V.L., Simauchi, K.A. (2021, October 15). Harvard's endowment soars to $53.2 billion, reports 33.6% returns. The Harvard Crimson. https://www.thecrimson.com/article/2021/10/15/endowment-returns-soar-2021/

5 Bennett, G., Lomax, M., & Ceuvas, K. How a $100M donation is a game-changer for HBCUs. PBS News Hour. https://www.pbs.org/newshour/show/how-a-100m-donation-is-a-game-changer-for-hbcus#:~:text=The%20United%20Negro%20College%20Fund%20has%20received%20a%20%24100%20million,in%20its%2080%2Dyear%20history

6 The White House. (2024, May 16). FACT SHEET: Biden-Harris Administration announces record over $16 billion in support for Historically Black Colleges and Universities (HBCUs). https://www.whitehouse.gov/briefing-room/statements-releases/2024/05/16/fact-sheet-biden-harris-administration-announces-record-over-16-billion-in-support-for-historically-black-colleges-and-universities-hbcus

7 Rosen, J. (2017, April 5). Black students who have at least one Black teacher are more likely to graduate. Johns Hopkins University. https://hub.jhu.edu/2017/04/05/black-teachers-improve-student-graduation-college-access/

8 Gershenson, S., Hart, C.M.D., Hyman, J., Lindsay, C.A., & Papageorge, N. (2022). The long-run impacts of same-race teachers. American Economic Journal: Economic Policy, 14(4), 300–342.

9 Mays, B.E. (1967, May 30). Twenty-seven years of success and failure at Morehouse College: Centennial Commencement Address 1967. Morehouse College Vertical Files. http://hdl.handle.net/20.500.12322/auc.141:0005

Black Students Can and Will Learn at Grace James and DuBois Academies
1 Dossett, D. (2023). Grace James Assessment Data.

*Kentucky Department of Education. School report card: Grace M. James Academy of Excellence. https://*www.kyschoolreportcard.com/organization/156433/academic_performance/assessment

performance/state_assessments_enrollment?year=2023

2 Owens, J. (2022). Double jeopardy: Teacher biases, racialized organizations, and the production of racial/ethnic disparities in school discipline. American Sociological Review, 87(6), 1007-1048. https://doi.org/10.1177/00031224221135810

3 Dossett, D. (2023). W.E.B. DuBois Assessment Data.

4 Kentucky Department of Education. School report card: W.E.B. DuBois Academy. https://www.kyschoolreportcard.com/organization/155129/academic_performance/assessment_performance/state_assessments_enrollment?year=2023

As It Relates — Black Louisville and Racial Equity; The Less and More of the Racial Equity Policy
1 Jefferson County Public Schools. (n.d). Equity Scorecard. https://assessment.jefferson.kyschools.us/DMC/ee/eeHome

2 This and additional JCPS racial equity documents can be accessed here: https://drive.google.com/drive/folders/195D03Tt2cxl_BVnXDHfdGvGGJOcGP0Sm?usp=sharing

The State of the District 2024
1 Baldwin, J. (1961). The Negro in American Culture; No. 3; The Negro Writer In America; Part 1. Boston, MA: The Walter J. Brown Media Archives & Peabody Awards Collection at the University of Georgia, Boston, MA; American Archive of Public Broadcasting (GBH and the Library of Congress), Boston, MA and Washington, DC. http://americanarchive.org/catalog/cpb-aacip-526-901zc7ss52

2 Prismatic Services, Incorporated. (2024, October). School district of Jefferson County Public Schools: An assessment of the transportation program and the transportation activities of August 9, 2023. https://s3.documentcloud.org/documents/24512614/v_a_jcpsphase1report_0-1.pdf

HEALTH

Anti-Racist and White: What DEP Offers to Address White Supremacy
1 Jefferson County Public Schools. (n.d.). Racial Equity Policy resource site. https://sites.google.com/jefferson.kyschools.us/jcpsracialequitypolicyhandbook

Food Justice and Farming in Louisville
1 U.S. Bureau of Labor Statistics. (2020, May 13). Unemployment rate rises to record high 14.7 percent in April 2020. https://www.bls.gov/opub/ted/2020/unemployment-rate-rises-to-record-high-14-point-7-percent-in-april-2020.htm

Parenting While Black
1 Condon, E.M., Barcelona, V., Ibrahim, B.B., Crusto, C.A., & Taylor, J.Y. (2022). Racial discrimination, mental
health, and parenting among African American mothers of preschool-age children. Journal of American Academy of Child Adolescent Psychiatry, 61(3), 402-412.

2 deMaat, D.A., Jansen, P.W., Prinzie, P., Keizer, R., Franken, I.H.A., & Lucassen, N. (2021). Examining longitudinal relations between mothers' and fathers' parenting stress, parenting behaviors, and adolescents'
behavior problems. Journal of Child and Family Studies, 30(3), 771-783.

The State of Environmental Justice
1 Squires, G.D., Gilderbloom, J.H., & Meares, W. (2020, July 21). Pollution, place, and the unnecessary tragedy of premature death: Lessons for Covid-19. Shelter Force. https://shelterforce.org/2020/07/21/pollution-place-and-the-unnecessary-tragedy-of-premature-death-lessons-for-covid-19/

2 Detrow, S., Ryan, E., & Ermyas, T. (2024, February 5). 'People do avoid me': How a toxic train derailment split a village in two. NPR. https://www.npr.org/2024/02/05/1228772709/east-palestine-train-derailment-norfolk-southern-lawsuit-epa

3 Magin, S., & Garcia, J. (2023, August 5). Chemical leak at west Louisville wastewater treatment plant; Here's what we know. WHAS11. https://www.whas11.com/article/news/local/chemical-spill-west-louisville-msd-pumping-station/417-3fb5272d-d576-43f1-8fe8-b1edf7f36a87

4 Environmental Protection Agency. (n.d.) TRI Toxics Tracker. https://edap.epa.gov/public/extensions/TRIToxicsTracker/TRIToxicsTracker.html

5 Strategic Toxic Air Reduction Program. (2007, September 19). Strategic toxic air reduction

regulation 5.30 stakeholder group report and plan of action. https://louisvilleky.gov/air-pollution-control-district/document/september-2007-strategic-toxic-air-reduction-star

6 Bullard, R.D. (2019, February 22). *African Americans on the frontline fighting for environmental justice.* https://drrobertbullard.com/african-americans-on-the-frontline-fighting-for-environmental-justice/

7 Baldwin, J. (1998). *Tell Me How Long the Train's Been Gone.* Penguin Books.

HOUSING

Louisville Needs More Housing Diversity

1 Greenberg, C. (2023, October 3; updated 2024, March 20). *My Louisville home: A comprehensive housing Strategy for a connected, healthy, authentic, sustainable, equitable and safe city.* https://louisvilleky.gov/housing/document/finalized-my-louisville-home

2 Louisville Metro Government. (2020, November 19). *An ordinance amending sections 92.02, 92.03, and 93.04 of the Louisville Metro Code of Ordinances ("LMCO") amending the discrimination ordinance providing for more fair access to rental housing (amendment by substitution).* https://louisville.legistar.com/LegislationDetail.aspx?ID=4700535&GUID=673B-DA87-E604-43C9-BDDB-EA165DA7ABA4&FullText=1

3 Kentucky General Assembly. (2024, March 6). *HB 18: An act relating to the rights of property owners and declaring an emergency.* https://apps.legislature.ky.gov/recorddocuments/bill/24RS/hb18/bill.pdf

4 Louisville Metro Government. (2019, January 1). *Plan 2040: A comprehensive plan for Louisville Metro.* https://louisvilleky.gov/planning-design/document/plan2040louisvillemetrocomprehensive-planfinal11-1-18pdf

5 Louisville Metro Government. (2021). *Land development code reform: Confronting inequities in land use policies, regulations and practices.* https://louisvilleky.gov/planning-design/document/ldc-reform-recommendations-summary-chart-2-1-21

6 Kentucky General Assembly. (2024, March 26). *House Concurrent Resolution 68: A concurrent resolution directing the establishment of the Kentucky Housing Task Force.* https://apps.legislature.ky.gov/record/24rs/hcr68.html

7 Kentucky General Assembly. (n.d.). *Special committee: Kentucky Housing Task Force.* https://legislature.ky.gov/Committees/Pages/Committee-Details.aspx?CommitteeRSN=425&CommitteeType=Special%2BCommittee

8 Kentucky General Assembly. (2024, January 9). *House Bill 102: An act relating to housing opportunities.* https://apps.legislature.ky.gov/record/24rs/hb102.html

9 Kentucky General Assembly. (2024, January 2). *House Bill 76: An act relating to rights and obligations of landlords and tenants to a residential lease.* https://apps.legislature.ky.gov/record/24rs/hb76.html

10 Kentucky General Assembly. *House Bill 466: An act relating to real property purchased at a master commissioner's sale.* https://apps.legislature.ky.gov/record/24rs/hb466.html

11 Kentucky General Assembly. *House Bill 388: An act relating to local government and declaring an emergency.* https://apps.legislature.ky.gov/record/24rs/hb388.html

Redressing Wealth Disparities Caused by Institutional Racism in Housing

1 Sullivan, B., Hays, D., & Bennett, N. (2024, April 23). *Households with a white, non-Hispanic householder were ten times wealthier than those with a Black householder in 2021.* U.S. Census Bureau. https://www.census.gov/library/stories/2024/04/wealth-by-race.html#:~:text=In%202021%2C%20households%20with%20a,only%204.7%25%20of%20all%20wealth.

2 Yun, L., Lautz, J., Evangelou, N., Snowden, B., & Dunn, M. (2023). *Snapshot of race and home buying in America.* National Association of Realtors. https://www.nar.realtor/sites/default/files/documents/2023-snapshot-of-race-and-home-buying-in-the-us-03-02-2023.pdf

The Fair Housing Act is Not Working

1 U.S. Department of Justice. (updated 2023, June 22). *The Fair Housing Act.* https://www.justice.gov/crt/fair-housing-act-1

2 Yun, L., Lautz, J., Snowden, B., & Dunn, M. (2024). *Snapshot of race and home buying in America*. National Association of Realtors. https://www.nar.realtor/sites/default/files/documents/2024-snapshot-of-race-and-home-buying-in-america-02-20-2024.pdf

3 Weekly, F. (2023, August 23). *Addressing the racial homeownership gap in Louisville*. Federal Reserve Bank of St. Louis. https://www.stlouisfed.org/publications/bridges/2023/vol3/addressing-racial-homeownership-gap-louisville

4 U.S. Department of Justice. (updated 2023, June 22). *The Fair Housing Act*. https://www.justice.gov/crt/fair-housing-act-1

5 Metropolitan Housing Committee; University of Louisville Center for Environmental Policy & Management. (2022). *State of metropolitan housing report: Towards a just housing future in uncertain times*. https://metropolitanhousing.org/wp-content/uploads/2022/06/2022-SMHR_FINAL.pdf

BLACK BUSINESS

Accelerators Are Not Enough to Address Black Wealth Disparities

1 King, E. (2022, September 27). *Black-owned businesses struggle to thrive in Kentuckiana*. WHAS11. https://www.whas11.com/article/news/local/black-owned-businesses-kentuckiana-kentucky-louisville/417-06c17df4-f187-40ab-80db-52fcff10cf04

Louisville Must Grow Our Economy Through Education, Emphasizing Business Opportunities and Future Workforce

1 Gardner, H. (2020, December 14). '200 years behind': Racial wealth gap impedes Black business ownership in Louisville." *Louisville Courier Journal*. https://www.courier-journal.com/in-depth/news/local/2020/12/14/black-louisville-business-owners-start-behind-due-to-wealth-gap/6507785002/

Investing in the Future of Black Business

1 Sasso, M. (2020, June 8). *Black business owners' ranks collapse by 41% in U.S. lockdowns*. Bloomberg. https://www.bloomberg.com/news/articles/2020-06-08/black-business-owners-suffer-41-drop-in-covid-19-lockdowns

2 Louisville Metro Government. (2021, July 2). *Mayor outlines added support for Black, minority-owned businesses*. https://louisvilleky.gov/news/mayor-outlines-added-support-black-minority-owned-businesses

3 A Path Forward for Louisville. (2020, June 19). https://apathforward4lou.org/

4 Perry, A.M., & Romer, C. (2020, December 31). *To expand the economy, invest in Black businesses*. The Brookings Institution. https://www.brookings.edu/articles/to-expand-the-economy-invest-in-black-businesses/

5 Bhutta, N., Chang, A.C., Dettling, L.J.., Hsu, J.W., & Hewitt, J. (2020, September 28). *Disparities in wealth by race and ethnicity in the 2019 Survey of Consumer Finances*. Board of Governors of the Federal Reserve System. https://doi.org/10.17016/2380-7172.2797

FURTHER REFLECTIONS

A Demonstration of Philanthropy and Black Communities as Strategic Partners and Champions for Transformative Change

1 Community Foundation of Louisville. (n.d.). *Invest Louisville*. https://www.cflouisville.org/invest-louisville/

2 A Path Forward for Louisville. (2020, June 19). https://apathforward4lou.org/

The Conviction to Champion Equity: Philanthropy's Role in Empowering Leaders of Color

1 Jolly, Pamela. (2020). *BLPP: The business case for investing in Black led social & economic change*. Torch Enterprises Inc.

2 Metro United Way. (n.d.). *Black L.O.V.E. Philanthropic Partnership*. https://metrounitedway.org/program/black-l-o-v-e-philanthropic-partnership/

3 Jolly, Pamela. (2020). *BLPP: The business case for investing in Black led social & economic change*. Torch Enterprises Inc.

Louisville
Urban League

2024

STATE OF BLACK LOUISVILLE

www.ingramcontent.com/pod-product-compliance
Lightning Source LLC
Chambersburg PA
CBHW042135120726
47911CB00022B/61
9780999883150